FROM FIRST PRINCIPLES

FROM FIRST PRINCIPLES

An Experiment in Ageing

Haim Hazan

Bergin & Garvey
Westport, Connecticut • London

94119

Library of Congress Cataloging-in-Publication Data

Hazan, Haim.
    From first principles : an experiment in ageing / Haim Hazan.
       p.   cm.
    Includes bibliographical references and index.
    ISBN 0–89789–462–6 (alk. paper)
    1. Aged—Great Britain—Attitudes. 2. Aged—Great Britain—Social
conditions. 3. Aging—Great Britain. 4. University of the Third
Age (Cambridge, England)   I. Title
HQ1064.G7H39   1996
305.26'0941—dc20   95–34301

British Library Cataloguing in Publication Data is available.

Library of Congress Catalog Card Number: 95–34301
ISBN: 0–89789–462–6

First published in 1996

Bergin & Garvey, 88 Post Road West, Westport, CT 06881
An imprint of Greenwood Publishing Group, Inc.

Printed in the United States of America

∞™

The paper used in this book complies with the
Permanent Paper Standard issued by the National
Information Standards Organization (Z39.48–1984).

10 9 8 7 6 5 4 3 2 1

For my wife, Mercia

Contents

Part II

TEXT:
SOUNDINGS OF THE CODE OF AGEING

Part III

CONTEXT:
TESTING OUT FOR AGEING

Acknowledgements

"From first principles" was a phrase frequently used by members of The University of the Third Age in Cambridge, England, while stressing their pursuit of the irreducible fundamentals of human existence. In that sense the presence of a younger foreigner among them invoked neither estrangement nor resentment. What seemed to me the added value of being an anthropologist—an identity apparently straddling cultural differences—proved to be a disadvantage. The members rejected outright any notion of cultural relativism and dismissed the value of conceptualization. Rather, they advocated the universal and the authentic. "The thing in itself" was both a desire and a reality whose unravelling represented the true quest for knowledge. Doing anthropology is primarily about doing justice to the point of view of "the native" and the people under this study resisted any patronizing stance debunking them of what they considered as their sole prerogative to express their own outlook. For this insistence I am immensely indebted. It urged me to rethink some of the run-of-the-mill conventions of anthropological rhetoric. The result is a presentation that is faithful to the intimate grammar of the members' world and voice, yet is informed and sustained by socio–anthropological lingo. The reflective effect of the contrast between the two sets the agenda for the composition of the book. The structure of the following, therefore, is a tribute to the order of classifications and priorities propounded by the members. It takes the reader on the bandwagon of anthropological discourse, travelling on a course set and signposted by the natives. For this experiment in anthropology and for the opportunity of getting acquainted with a congenial, hospitable, and wise group of women and men, I am very grateful.

The person whose initiative and support opened this opportunity to me is Professor P. Laslett of Trinity College, Cambridge, who, in his capacity as chairperson of the organization, saw the need and significance of studying it and introduced me to its members. Professor Laslett also read a draft of the manuscript and offered some useful comments.

The critical remarks made by Professors Z. Bauman and C. Silver contributed a great deal to the development of the argument.

I am particularly indebted to Mr. A. Raz, my student and colleague, whose insightful contribution to the preparation of the manuscript is invaluable to the text.

The Faculty of Social Sciences at Tel-Aviv University, The Brookdale Institute of Gerontology and Adult Human Development in Jerusalem, and the Bar-Ilan Brookdale program, all assisted in funding various stages of the project.

Far beyond the perfunctory call of duty, I would like to express my thanks to my wife, Mercia, whose unbending faith in the unorthodox approach I adopted in this study gave me the strength and conviction to carry it through.

Tel-Aviv, 1996

Preface

The study of ageing is dominated by the non-aged. This simple fact, most of the time taken for granted, covers a Pandora's box of commonplace, stereotypes, practical know-how, and sociological conceptions, all devised to render the aged into a culturally reified symbolic category that is socially accountable, yet sequestered from society. By and large, the host of knowledge on ageing produced by the non-aged is deemed to retain—and sustain—the difference in perspective on the borderline between life and death, as construed, respectively, by those on its verge and those desperate to avoid it.

It was, therefore, exciting and promising when a group of elderly persons in The University of the Third Age in Cambridge, England, offered themselves to serve as a living laboratory for the study of ageing. Arguably the first institution of its kind in Britain, The University of the Third Age in Cambridge has become, due to its novelty, its founder Peter Laslett, and its success in terms of membership, a trend-setter for other similar establishments. What caught my attention, however, was not so much the administrative accomplishments of this project, but its members' success in using the educational format of its courses and discussion groups in order to rethink, from first principles, their view of the world.

Faced with the daunting prospects of decrepitude, deterioration, and dependency and being relatively fit and alert for the present, these people could be said to have conducted an undeclared experiment in ageing. Like any other experiment, it did not commit the people involved, nor did it immediately change their lives. It did, however, brace them with an a-priori knowledge of things to come and of possible ways and means of coping.

The intellectual experiment conducted within the University of the Third Age (the U3A, as its members call it) was set to examine critically, and refute, a whole spectrum of socio-cultural premises concerning the understanding of human behaviour. To begin with, doubts and misgivings were evoked about the very possibility of social scientists getting to grips with ageing. It was argued that the analytic devices, academic terminology, and conceptual frameworks at the disposal of sociologists and anthropologists are inadequate to study the phenomenon of ageing. There exists a basic incongruity between the model of ageing as constructed by both scientific and everyday language and its actual, "real" experience. What is needed, then, is no less than a new language, a new mode of articulation capable of capturing the essentials of human existence.

As a long-time anthropologist of old age, for me this genuine experiment was both alarming and eye-opening—alarming, as it put to the question the very validity of applying scientific terms of reference in the understanding of old age, and eye-opening as it threw into relief the issue of the "otherness" of the aged, demonstrating that the fabric of their world is still comprehensible and communicable. It only needs to be observed, so I understood, with a third-age eye. It is with such a "third-age eye" that one must read the verbal texts transcribed from the meetings of the discussion group that are examined throughout the book. These are texts of mixed historical and mythical images, such as of Red Indians, ancient Egyptians, and Oxbridge dons, all seemingly garbled and incoherent. Yet they incorporate a logic of their own, a logic of experimentation with a new form of language, perhaps even a new "Logos."

The paradigm of experiment—recently challenged and redefined by both modern physics (with its uncertainty principle) and reflexive anthropology (with its participant observation)—should also serve to introduce some of the problematics underlying the project both of the elderly participants and of this book. Experiments are designed within controlled conditions to access the unfamiliar by means of the familiar, thereby transferring the latter into the former. Yet what our experiment really demonstrates is that disturbing and insoluble incompatibility between concepts and phenomena—the academic perspective versus the "native" point of view, and ultimately the perspectives of "us" and "them." The employment of the language of experiment, then, stems from an attempt to constitute a channel of communication between the two languages, that of academic discourse and the actual experience of the elderly in the U3A. Its difficulty, perhaps awkwardness, testifies to the author's Sisyphean toil of attempting to reconcile these antitheticals. And, indeed, Sisyphean it was for the experimenters, who were engaged in a constant and implausible exercise of mixing and distilling modes of articulating the world.

Moreover, the use of "experiment" as a paradigmatic frame of reference aspires to do justice to the spirit of the elderly persons in question, whose outlook on the world was scientific—even though, as we shall learn, their intellectual efforts were directed towards analysing and decomposing rather than synthesizing and reconstructing. In some way it is a tribute to and an extension of the pursuit of the literal and the fundamental as manifested by the people under study, rather than an expression of metaphor and representation so frequently employed to touch upon ageing. This endeavour—to be faithful to the model of the observed and not that of the observer—might well result in some peculiar and self-contradictory arguments. The reader should be the natural judge of the cogency and usefulness of these presentations.

PART I

DISCOURSE:
ASSUMPTIONS OF AGEING

. . . The steam is living breath. It was water; now it goes up to the sky, becomes a cloud again. These things are sacred. We have a saying that the white man sees so little, he must see with only one eye. . . . But we, we live in a world of symbols and images where the spiritual and commonplace are one.

[John Fire Lame Deer, an old Sioux shaman,
quoted in Bunge 1984:83]

Life could be compared to an embroidery of which we see the right side during the first half of life, but the back in the latter half. This back side is less scintillating but more instructive: it reveals the interpatterning of the threads.

[Schopenhauer 1844:215]

We are all pretty antique, and we can all think back to the moments when on quite important things we thought again from first principles, and changed. Even if it's only the colour of the bedroom curtains.

[One of the members of The University
of the Third Age in Cambridge]

CHAPTER 1

Substance:
A Question of Learning

During one of the general meetings of the U3A, when the agenda for future activities was set and contacts with other learning institutions were discussed, a member of the audience heckled the speaker and exclaimed: "What is the point of this discussion anyway, they can't understand us, they can't see the world like we do, with a third-age eyesight."

This intriguing statement about the implausibility of communicating with the non-old met with "hear, hear" murmurs of approval from the floor, and was in turn adopted as a local locution suggesting the uniqueness of the point of view of the elderly. This whole book can be regarded as an attempt to understand and explain what lies behind the plea "to see things with a third-age eye." The reader, then, should be prepared for a short organized tour in the land of the "third-age" people.

As the experiment in ageing conducted by the aged in The University of the Third Age is unfolded, it will be shown to provide a model case where culture is dismantled and the stark basis of human articulation is exposed. The interpretation of the spoken texts offered by the elderly participants, to be pursued in the middle part of the book, will undoubtedly provide some of the windings that await down the road. But the rare landscape viewed from that passage—"the first principles," in the words of U3A members, to be abstracted from the "debris" of one's cultural and personal life—should pay for the effort. Let us first describe, in some detail, the field of study and its inhabitants.

The University of the Third Age can be seen to consist of three concentric circles of relevant inquiry. At the circumference we encounter the macro-structure of socio-cultural forces. The second, middle circle consists of the institutional context of the university. It defines the circumstantial provisions whose understanding interconnects the first circle with the third, whose radial is the social interaction taking place within the boundaries of our setting.

Part and parcel of this social interaction, and indeed a much discussed one in recent anthropological literature, is the interaction of researcher and researchees. Taken to the extreme, it can be argued that the only authentic data available for ethnographic discourse concerns interaction between the researcher and the "other."[1] It should be noted that such interactions are deliberately placed beyond the scope of this account, since the focus of our interest lies exclusively in the social products of the elderly in question. This is by no means a denial of the role of the anthropologist as an instigator or promoter of social action. However, in the relationship between the world of the elderly and the temporary impact of the anthropologist on its shaping, the balance is heavily and consciously tipped towards the former.

The following relates the general model of the three circles to our subject matter. One of the significant frames of reference of this study is the exploration of a new mode of old-age related literacy. Hence the macroscopic–structural circle should encompass the socio-cultural meaning given in contemporary society to learning in later life. The second circle refers to the organizational and institutional arrangements that set the practical scene for such learning to take place, namely Universities of the Third Age in general and the one in Cambridge in particular. The inner, microscopic circle includes the actually observed field of people, situations and interactions.

It was Irvin Rosow (1974) who, in a seminal sociological treatise of the socially structured position of the old in modern society, challenged the unspoken premise that while the young must undergo institutionalized procedures of socialization in order to be integrated into society, the old, having no such facilities, are at a dead end. This impasse entails three problematics: the old are put into a statusless, purposeless social position with neither approval nor direction; society itself faces a lacuna, a vacuum devoid of roles and channels of mobility; and the sociologist is conceptually empty-handed and intellectually mystified while trying to decipher the meaning of such existence. A few noteworthy attempts have been made to reach beyond the plaster of social stereotypes and the zone of "social problems," to touch upon the meaning old people attach to their lives.[2] However, questions of "coping," "competence," "orientation," and "adjustment" usually remain within the scope of managing everyday life and not of making sense of it. Rosow's challenge of deciphering the means employed by the old as "socialization to old age" is still open to conjecture.

It is within this broad frame of reference that the subject of learning in old age should be considered. Evidence shows that the interest in and the preoccupation with all forms of study during old age is constantly increasing.[3] It should be noted, however, that I am not dealing here with the general subject of "adult education" participated in by "mature students." What I am examining is the more interesting state of those learners whose career prospects and social achievements can no longer profit from an involvement in courses of study. Partly as a result of their "retired" status, the learning facilities available to the old are either very general (such as the mass media) or specially designed frameworks (such as the U3A). Institutions for higher education such as universities, although not usually imposing any age barrier on their students, must be excluded from this spectrum, since admission is, in fact, reserved for those who are able to meet the formal requirements—that is, the young. Furthermore, being an age-homogenous environment, universities informally construct youth sub-cultures.

Our discussion does not intend to address the complicated debate as to the decline or otherwise in learning abilities throughout the life span and particularly during the later years. Whether elderly people experience a gradual drop in their intellectual capacities of reasoning and short-term memory, as Bromley (1974) suggests or as others proclaim,[4] the commonly held preconception regarding the deterioration in learning abilities should be perceived as yet another social myth emanating from both prejudice and misconceived aptitude tests. As Midwinter (1982:66), in his incisive analysis of the issue of learning in old age, states:

> In the last analysis it does not matter a jot whether in the conventional and measurable sense the elderly are able or unable to learn. If memories fail, if reactions slow to the minimal, if problem-solving were found to be impossible, it would not, from a standpoint of objective, matter. The one question is whether or not the activity is life-enhancing . . . the chief, perhaps the sole purpose, is the self-esteem, the satisfaction to be gained by the individuals and the enabling of them to realize their "best self."

LEARNING IN OLD AGE
AS A RESEARCH SETTING

Before offering our own version of "life enhancement" and "best self," it seems important to sketch out a few of the constituents of the dilemma of learning in old age. This dilemma stems from the fact that institutionalized learning in old age cannot be seen to function as a regular means of socialization or of attaining a higher occupational, professional, or social status, in the way that educational institutions usually do. What, then, is the motivation that older people share in their involvement in learning that does not serve any economic or professional function? The goal of acquiring knowledge in old age, if knowledge is indeed acquired, is not clear. Several reasonable causes might evidently be broached to answer the problem, and some of them will even receive affirmation from the learners' own proclaimed stances. The answer, however, would prove to be much more complicated.

1. The intellectual desire to broaden one's horizons, disregarding one's age, may be raised as a general explanation. However, personal learning is well sufficient for this purpose. Such reasoning does not account for the social character of institutional learning.

2. Knowledge acquisition is a socially approved sign of mental agility and intellectual power. Thus, older people can take advantage of their proclaimed learning activity as a protection against stereotypical accusations of mental frailty, dementia, and general incompetence.

3. The process of acquiring knowledge usually involves social interaction and thus helps to develop and sustain skills of communication and to provide opportunities for social exchange. Engaging in peer-group learning can provide the elderly, often robbed by retirement of their previous roles, relations, and social engagements, with a means of attaining new ones. Regaining social relations and participation in such a peer group may also serve as compensation for negative self- and social image.

4. Involvement in such an organized and regular activity can serve to fill the lacunae of free time facing the retired person and perhaps substitute for his previous engagement at work.

Knowledge, being the invaluable resource that it is, lends itself to tight social control. In pre-literate cultural settings where the dissemination of knowledge was orally channelled, or in societies in which the lack of technical means such as printing did not permit general exposure to knowledge, rigid boundaries of accessible literacy or promoted ignorance were set. Such means of control are rendered effective when knowledge can be differentially appropriated to designated social groups or categories according to their respective standings in the social system. However, in a multimedia modern society such checks and balances become loose, and the allocation of knowledge is not necessarily compatible with the prevalent power structures. Markers separating areas of available knowledge from forbidden zones of imposed ignorance nonetheless still exist, but they are made of more subtle and less obtrusive cultural materials—such as class-related linguistic codes,[5] implicit rules of inclusion and exclusion,[6] and age-allied stereotypes. This last instance is, indeed, the cause of the intricate relationship between forms of social control of knowledge and the aged in our society. The construction of old age bars the elderly from gaining access to various services,[7] of which one is the availability and use of knowledge. Let us look into the properties of such enforced ignorance. It should be noted that an interesting parallel could be drawn between mandatory retirement, which constitutes the forfeiting of the right to socio-economic autonomy, and the denial of knowledge acquisition, which amounts to subjecting a whole category of persons to cultural stagnation and entropy. The structural factors responsible for such a state are common to both phenomena and, indeed, to the whole concept of old age in highly industrialized societies.

The social vacuum created by the absence of role-based social identities in old age is filled with alternative media of cultural knowledge, namely social stereotypes. These units of pseudo-information form and shape conceptions and taken-for-granted beliefs about the category of the old as an indivisible homogenous collectivity. They serve to preserve and reinforce existing social conditions and to uphold the interests of the non-old to keep away from the old. Thus, the dependency of the old on the rest of society is maintained. The key stereotypical image that furnishes this need and from which other images spring is probably the one depicting the old as conservative, non-creative people who resist change and are reluctant and unable to adjust themselves to new circumstances. Learning, being the main vehicle for altering consciousness and redirecting the course of one's life, is at the hub of this image. Hence, old people are conceived of as incapable of learning, and this attribute supposedly accounts for their social and personal stagnation. This image reveals itself in a host of manifestations, varying from the culturally pervasive lesson of the trite adage "you can't teach an old dog new tricks" to the highly institutionalized labelling process of discrediting elderly persons as "senile," "mentally frail," or "demented." It is, indeed, the confusion between the normal and the pathological that intensifies the stigmatic effect of observable "maladjustment" among the old. Scientists' exhortations to differentiate between the two so that the pathological does not inform our view of the normal remain unheeded in research (see, e.g., Birren & Munnichs 1983) and certainly in popular belief. The capacity to learn, as defined and formulated in tests and reflected in graded scales of measuring aptitudes and determining life chances, is devised by and designed for the non-aged—a fact that in itself attests to the biased view held with regard to the nature and quality of learning. Therefore, when such a discriminatory, ageistic yardstick is applied to the aged, it becomes a self-fulfilling prophecy, since its expectations exclude ambivalence, non-linear thinking, and the input of personal experience.[8] Thus, elderly people are relegated by both scientists and lay-people to the dubious status of "old-age pensioners," entailing an imputed learning deficiency.

This mechanism of social control is sustained by age-norms that regulate and supervise the gates of education for all members of society. In the case of the aged, such gates are formally or informally closed. This rule is, of course, inverted when it comes to the young: in their case, the gates of education constitute a mandatory framework of socialization. The dominant regulation of pedagogic discourse has indeed been described by many authors (see, e.g., Bourdieu & Passeron 1970; Apple 1982; Bernstein 1990). Interestingly, the conventional term taken to denote education in general—namely "pedagogy"—in fact literally means "the art and science of teaching children" (in Greek, *paed* = child). This etymological slant, which had come to stand for a social one, has caused some authors (see, e.g., Dubois 1975:189) to coin a counter-concept, "andragogy" (derived from Greek *andr* = man). In contrast to the millennia of research (and hopefully some progress) made in the field of pedagogy, the following comment by Howard McClusky (1971) spells an opposite picture with regard to andragogy:

> When we search the world of scholarship for "hard data" related to the education of older people, we emerge from our inquiry with several substantial impressions. First, such data on the education of older persons is extremely limited: obviously, this is a domain much neglected by educational research. Second, with respect to the amount of formal education attained, older persons are extremely disadvantaged.

Since some reference must be made to the accrued knowledge of the elderly, its ascribed worthlessness is euphemistically described as "personal experience," "reminiscence," and "life stories," whose importance rests with the supposed cultural legacy that it keeps in store for future generations. In fact, the elderly are reduced to becoming members of an almost extinct species, that of story-tellers whose credibility in our society, being previously based on a no longer valid oral tradition, is only humoured and dismissed. In a society where a strict separation prevails between the source of knowledge, knowledge itself, and the receiver of knowledge, the reunification of the three is inconceivable. Yet elderly persons are deemed to be identified with their messages and are thus rendered incompatible with conventional modes of the production, dissemination, and reliable control of knowledge. Regarded as non-verifiable, idiosyncratic and irrelevant, knowledge produced by the old, therefore, is not counted as a valuable social resource, just as the aged themselves are considered ineligible for learning.

Since career-oriented knowledge is incongruent with the stereotype of being old, the elderly are not only discouraged from participating in institutions for learning, but are also expected to reaffirm those images by voluntarily preoccupying themselves in settings and subjects befitting their "appropriate" social position. Be it in sheltered settings, such as institutions, pensioners' clubs, or day centres, or within the community at large, recreational facilities and study classes mirror an image of the old as being in constant pursuit of hobbies, voluntary work, games of chance, and sheer sociability.

The conception of time—considered a valuable resource in our society and measured in terms of scarcity, efficiency, and, above all, utility (see, e.g., Roy 1959; Roth 1962; Maxwell 1972; Zerubavel 1985)—also plays an interesting role in the designation of such activities as more appropriate to old age. Within the normal, adult-world conception of time, courses of study are designed as stages in a pre-planned career trajectory pursued by the student. They are defined and divided as temporal units within a broader, linear time perspective. Socially rewarded learning, therefore, is a culturally constructed structuring device and as such is subjected to the rules governing the management of time in our society. There are, however, units of time that are precluded from the linear flow of career tracks and future-geared designations. These are the cyclical modes which can take many shapes and forms, such as ritual (see Leach 1971; Moore & Myerhoff 1977), habit,[9] and leisure.[10] It is intriguing to note the relation between these forms of activity and old age.

The elderly retirees are treated as a leisure class. Time is deemed to be abundantly at their disposal and the choice of non-career activities limitless. These cultural assumptions are reflected in the character of pastimes designed for and offered to elderly persons. This view is intensified when engaging the old in activities for their own sake is thought of as having a therapeutic effect—hence the range of non-remunerative, non-instrumental assignments of occupational therapy. Another expression of this view can be found in the subject-matter composing the curricula of education for the elderly. These are premised on the association between the presumed past-oriented mentality of the aged and their expected areas of interest. Thus classes in history, archaeology, literature, and art are more commonly offered in such courses than physics, mathematics, and technical matters, albeit with the exception of "do-it-yourself" and gardening. Further support for this preferred choice of courses is provided by an assumption that the aged are incapable of having a "modern" frame of mind and of grasping issues that are at the fore of science and whose understanding presumably requires the application of precise sequential, logical modes of reasoning.

All these structural constraints seem to narrow greatly the spectrum of learning opportunities open to the aged. However, if indeed the substantive materials of learning serve no apparent interest and, in fact, only help to strengthen social images of the aged, what is the underlying intentionality in attending classes and courses of study for the elderly? This book is not intent on offering a general answer to this question, nor is it set to explore comparatively the various purposes and possibilities of learning in old age. Instead it presents the case of one group of elderly people who, through their words and actions, manifest the paradoxical nature of learning in old age.[11]

These elderly students have developed a mode of learning whose templates are not the substantive materials upon which the standardized acquisition of knowledge is based. Their andragogy was not designed to enhance the reservoir of available information, nor to develop career-pertinent skills. One of the postulates of that andragogical discourse was that the substance of study is immaterial to the methods devised to process it. This may account for the rather random choice of subjects selected by elderly learners and for the avoidance of areas of knowledge with built-in analysing procedures—such as the deductive sciences. The less rigidly structured the subject is, the more degrees of interpretative freedom it offers.

This type of learning invokes other examples where form, structure, and method override substance. Such are the scholastic Talmudic deliberations in orthodox Jewish culture, whose main concern is the consideration of analytic procedures and modes of formal extrapolation (Heilman 1983). The mastery of these methods is not conditional upon the specific material at hand, nor is it limited to a given social class.[12] It is open to the exercise of infinite intellectual capabilities within a guarded set of taken-for-granted—indeed "sacred"—principles and themes.

The elderly under study were determined to set no academic rules that could restrict intellectual freedom. Theirs was a quest for ultimate truths, for first principles. One could paraphrase Goody's (1977) illuminating study of the evolution of literacy, "The Domestication of the Savage Mind," and note that these elderly evince the reverse: the undomestication of the human mind. With this thought in mind, we will proceed to describe the field and the forms of inverted literacy produced by its incumbents. The ensuing discussion will, therefore, take us from a general discourse on ageing and andragogy to our specific field of study—namely, The University of the Third Age in Cambridge. The latter, as we shall further see, is by no means a passive manifestation of the former. However, its activities must be considered against that overarching social discourse, of which the members themselves were constantly aware and were perhaps only too alert to the possibility of being subjugated to.

THE U3A AS A SETTING
FOR LEARNING IN OLD AGE

The first thing that meets the eye in the U3A is its title. Let us therefore examine the trope of the "third age" as a possible doorway to the world of its university. Joining forces with the rest of society, the old themselves, while reaffirming and reinforcing some of the images attributed to them, contrive their own means of warding off the notion of finitude embedded in such social messages. In a secular society, where no spiritual comfort or intellectual explanation can be offered to the phenomenon of non-life, such a barrier is vital for the perpetuation of everyday life without facing the devastating realization of its imminent termination. The reluctance of old people to be associated with the very old or the physically infirm and the mentally frail among themselves (see, e.g., Hazan 1992) is one testimony to the erections of such walls. Other evidence that concerns us here is the invention of the concept of the "third age," a term approved of by many of the elderly and endorsed by a variety of social agents dealing with the old. This collaboration springs from the common interest in the need to delineate a demarcation line between life and death.

The culturally entrenched trope of the "four ages of man,"[13] with its self-evident seasonal connotation, places the third age between the "second age" of procreational, productive mid-life and the "fourth age" of debilitation and final decline (Keith 1980). Verging both on a caste-like social entity of outcasts and on a class-like construction of socio-economic powerlessness, the category of the third age draws a multitude of cultural associations ranging from "limbo"[14] to "new pioneers" (Silverman 1987).

The setting of social boundaries for the category of the "old" as opposed to the "very old" spells the advent of a cultural formulation of the former as a stage in the life course. The intense interest of behavioural scientists in the developmental orbit of childhood and adolescence has been extended to adulthood and ageing[15] to form moulds of "natural," "taken-for-granted" clusters of social norms. Consequently, a body of academic knowledge concerning issues pertaining to the nature of this incipient phase in the life span is beginning to emerge and cultivate its own turf. As with so many other social phenomena, the act of spelling out is here also an act of reification.

One of the subjects that increasingly gains ground in the attempt to establish the profile of the third age is the concern with the properties of learning among the old. Since the concept of the third age patently means a distinction between "normal ageing" and "pathological ageing," the interest in cognitive processes and in the place of memory and experience in the life of the "normal aged" has shifted from the traditional preoccupation with the effect of old-age-related diseases on a mental impairment to age-associated changes in the mastery of aptitudes, skills, personality, and information processing. Once the unavoidable albeit irrelevant comparison between the performances of young and old is removed,[16] some intriguing findings could be ascertained.

Notwithstanding the significance of such new findings for the understanding of learning throughout the life span, they attest to the gradual inclusion of the elderly as consumers of knowledge into the educational supermarket of institutions, services, and facilities for learning. This process is heralded and formulated in ideological charter-statements advocating the rights of the old to a share in the intellectual profits of a highly literate society. The following principles (taken from Laslett 1984) are an example of such a manifesto for the old.

1. "A fair share of the budget."
2. "Education is not just for youth."
3. "Access to all institutions."
4. "National distance teaching."
5. "Cultural recognition."

Those tenets, self-explanatory as they are, embody an inherent contradiction between the clear demand for cultural recognition and subsequent social rights and an admission as to the nature and quality of the fulfilment of such needs. This dilemma is lucidly expressed in the summation of that charter:

> We are still largely ignorant of what the elderly should be taught, or teach themselves in order to give them that mental stimulation which they so much need and which may go some way towards keeping them from becoming expensive liabilities to the health and social services. But I believe that their ripeness, experience and wisdom fit them for a function of which we stand pre-eminently in need—the preservation and intensification of our cultural heritage. [Laslett 1984:27]

A mosaic of attributed needs, ascribed rights, and cultural commitment constitutes the message of this document and, indeed, reflects social quandaries regarding the organizational means, the appropriation of resources, and the channels of communication that should be deployed to satisfy those unclear objectives.

Alongside suggestions of integration into existing universities, developing adult education courses, and enhancing the use of the mass media for the purpose of teaching the old, the idea of a special framework for learning in the third age gathers accelerated momentum. The notion of a university for the third age was conceived and first implemented in Toulouse, France, in the summer of 1972, when Pierre Vellas, Professor of Political Economy, initiated *"L'Université du Troisième Age"* for retired persons. It took place on the unused premises of the local campus during the vacation and included lectures and a host of cultural activities. The idea, having caught up in many other European countries (Radcliffe 1984), has acquired the characteristics of a social movement whose spokespersons and advocates promote it as both an end unto itself and as part of a community-forming enterprise (Philibert 1984). For the purpose of our discussion, we shall confine the referential scope of the second circle—the organizational frame—to one prominent British manifestation of that general phenomenon.[17]

The extensive course of my participant observations in the U3A included interviews with a great number of members, attendance at social and official gatherings, active membership in the research committee of the U3A, gleaning of multifaceted documentation pertaining to the "field," and, last but not least, an intensive involvement in one particular study group whose declared objective was socio-anthropological knowledge. Each of these arenas warrants, and shall receive, a more detailed account of its contribution to the discussion.

The geographical distribution of the overall population under study—that is, the approximately 500 members of the U3A—did not allow for many identifications between residence and social interaction, and hence the restriction of observations to organized activities, occasional meetings, and planned interviews. Although most members dwell in the city and its suburbia, many come from far afield in the country, such as small towns and villages. In any case, there were no traceable interactional patterns interweaving the individuals partaking in the social world[18] of learning into a social network of multidimensional relationships. This is not to say that common interest did not reveal itself in the form of friendship, intimacy, and other extra-curricular shared engagements. However, the U3A as a research arena could be described and circumscribed only in terms of its core characteristic rather than as a distinct social unit. It can be stated that belonging to the organization constitutes a significant albeit not a dominant part in the lives of its members. The implications of this observation on the conduct of anthropological inquiry are far-reaching.

The need to direct attention to the properties of a common denominator such as learning spells the abandonment of one of the foremost tenets of anthropology, namely the holistic principle. It becomes both impossible and unnecessary—not to say impeding—to provide a fully fledged account of the lives of the people concerned or to articulate a report of a bounded social arena.

The holistic narrative of "writing culture" (Clifford & Marcus 1986) is hence replaced here with a more carefully focused anthropological plot. By avoiding the temptation to become submerged in life stories and/or histories[19] or in any form of "community-oriented" research,[20] this book seeks to follow only one, distinct logic of description—namely that connected with the articulation of a new world-view through the textual practices of learning and literacy. This meant that I had to put my emphasis on the texts rather than the people producing them. The interviewees' backgrounds and past experiences, interesting though they might have been, could have pushed the study to the byways of individual worlds.

My intention is to focus upon the verbal texts produced by the members of the U3A as a doorway to their world. Such a methodological and theoretical stance parallels the abandonment of context in recent anthropological studies of cultural texts.[21] Moreover, it meets with the approval of the U3A members themselves, who were well aware of the split in their life-worlds[22] and, indeed, welcomed the opportunity that old age has put in their way to dwell on multiple and separate identities. Rather than providing access to the speaker's overall identity,[23] these texts suggest a step beyond context towards deciphering the code of old age as perceived and formulated by elderly people. If successful, this attempt at decontextualizing old age might give the language of the old a hearing. The fact that the people under study were in relatively good health, financially secure, mentally alert, and socially respectable separated our case from problems commonly associated with old age, such as illness, destitution, and loss of status. What we have is an account of the expressed thoughts of elderly people whose acute awareness of old age is still free of its scourges.[24]

For the purposes of our inquiry, old age is examined neither in its socio-economic–demographic facets nor in its mental implications. To us, old age consists of its narratives[25] as told by the aged. As in any other narrative, the relationship between text on the one hand and context, content, and teller on the other is of a complex nature. The occasional authors of our texts are featured in this study in a fashion similar to that of writers undertaking a literary discussion of their works.[26] Evidently, the understanding of poetics could take cues from the biographical venue of authors and poets in the same way as the research into folk-tales can be related to, and benefits from, an acquaintance with the narrator. In both cases, however, the story, the tale, the poem, the song, the picture, or any other work of art could stand on its own as an object to comprehend and marvel at. The anthropological project as a means of attaining such appreciation of human conduct and cultural productions is particularly germane, albeit problematic, to the understanding of old age and accounts by the elderly. This is the subject of chapter 2.

CHAPTER 2

Analytic Considerations:
A Question of Anthropology

Anthropological authority has traditionally stemmed from the craft of presenting the voice of the "other" to, and into, academic discourse. This authority, textual or otherwise, has recently been challenged from various directions (see, e.g., Ruby 1982; Clifford 1983; Clifford & Marcus 1986; Sanjek 1990). The object of anthropology as a translation of cultural codes has been described by Asad (1986:161) as "not the historical situated speech (that is the task of the folklorist or the linguist) but 'culture,' and to translate culture the anthropologist must first read and then inscribe the implicit meanings that lie beneath/within/beyond situated speech." It is this ultimate accomplishment of translation through the unravelling of hidden agendas that justifies and constitutes the research method of participant observation developed by anthropologists to obtain knowledge of the "other" by the "other." However, Asad goes on to criticize that rather commonly invoked model of ethnography as translation, whose apparent "neutrality" is enmeshed in global-power inequalities of post-colonialism, modernization, capitalism, and cultural hegemony. There are persistently "strong" and "weak" languages, he acutely observes, and the vast majority of ethnographies are written in strong languages. Moreover, "cultures" are not coherent languages or texts but are themselves composed of many conflicting discourses.

The anthropology of ageing adds further dimensions to this criticism. Here, the gulf between the two protagonists of the research—the anthropologist and the "other"—is such that "othering," namely entering the other's world and viewing it from within, becomes frankly impossible. Unlike other ethnographic situations, the human condition of old age is inimitable and unprecedented in the course of one's life. The ageing-imputed experience of facing impending death, counting one's losses, and reviewing life distances the elderly from the "non-old," whose own experience is not fraught with such reckonings.

The epistemological lacunae inherent in all ethnography loom larger in the case of old age, inviting short-cuts in the form of pre- and misconceptions, briefly surveyed in chapter 1, and to which I dedicate a more thorough examination elsewhere (Hazan 1995). One conceivable solution for such a predicament could be offered by the aged themselves. The anthropologist, whose questionable knowledge regarding the state of being old does not allow for a credible translation of the language of ageing into an anthropological twang, can enlist the help of elderly persons in spelling out the principles of their own language. Putting the elderly in the position of vicarious anthropologists is not tantamount to the traditional role of the informant, where the right of reflexive conceptualization becomes the reserved privilege of the anthropologist once the roles are reversed and former hearer (field ethnographer) becomes speaker (anthropological author) while former speakers (informants) become spoken texts. If the argument put forward by some anthropologists that peer-group communication in old age produces new norms and novel meanings (Keith 1980) is valid, then elderly persons could be regarded as commentators of this unknown old-age-peculiar cultural edifice. This challenge, which must be met in order to ascertain the validity of any endeavour to make ageing audible, might be taken on by elderly students of old age whose reflexive faculties can do justice to the nature of their experience, hence transmitting it to the domain of the non-old.

Attempts towards an anthropological deciphering of the "exotic" world of the aged are numerous. If Victor Turner's (1978) dictum that the role of the ethnographer is "to exoticize the familiar and to familiarize the exotic" is to be considered a guideline for researchers, then the anthropologist is a translator not only of the language of folk-models into the language of analytic construction, but also vice-versa. He or she must invest resources other than academic to be able to straddle the two universes of researcher and researchee. This investment could be personal and subjective, by way of empathy and identification (see Myerhoff 1978; Crapanzano 1980), reserved and guarded to subscribe to the accepted codex of scientific investigation (see Kaufman 1986; Francis 1984), or strictly striving for objectivity premised on the belief in human universals, which bridge the gap between the "native" and his student. Any of these methods has to grapple with the dilemmas posed by trying to understand ageing as a phenomenon verging on incomprehensibility.

The scope of fundamental issues embedded in the study of ageing encompasses some of the most intriguing dilemmas looming on the horizons of our understanding. Many of those are eclipsed by convention and camouflaged by our own defences. The introduction of ageing as a source of knowledge infusing and illuminating such topics might prove to be an intellectual boon but an analytic bane. Deprived of conceptual frames to befit the phenomenon at hand (see Fabian 1983) and denied, by virtue of age-discrepancy, of the opportunity to share the experience of ageing with the "native," the anthropologist of old age is methodologically at a loss.

To illustrate this point, and before explicating its possible solution (adumbrated earlier), let us concisely enumerate some seemingly unanswerable questions broached by touching upon ageing:

1. *How to understand identity and cultural presence without their attributed insignia—namely socially allocated roles, which, in the case of elderly people, are usually stripped off.* Concepts of mobility, status, and stratification are analytically erroneous in a state where social rewards and sanctions are disassociated from procedures of exchange, mutuality and cumulativity.

2. *How to think of that subject in the anthropologically sacrosanct holistic fashion, when so many aspects of being old are diverse and compartmentalized and do not inform one another.* Body is divorced from mind, the physical does not answer to the mental, and vice versa (de Beauvoir 1975). The ageing self is split between its ageless properties and its rapidly and dramatically changing circumstances. Inner life is no longer furnished by external appearance (Neugarten 1977), and the composite self consisting of the subjective "I" and the social "me" (Mead 1934) is rendered divisible. Hence, the tacit cultural assumption sustained by anthropologists regarding the unity of the self does not withstand the scrutiny of an encounter with elderly people.

3. *How to relate to persons whose course of social mobility has come to an end and hence their yardsticks for assessing and constructing reality are fundamentally different from those held by the still socially mobile researcher.* Furthermore, this is not just a question of socially endorsed rewards and progress along the life cycle since it draws on significant transformations in conceptions of time, space, and meaning.

    Such changes may account for an unredeemable and irreversible breech of communication between the world of the anthropologist and that of the informants. Understanding the other under such conditions could be about grasping and comprehending nonpertinent matters while overlooking the hub of the phenomenon under study. Thus an illusion of knowledge could be mistaken for knowledge.

4. *How to reconcile the obvious universal properties of the process of ageing with cultural diversity and personal idiosyncrasies.* Is ageing a unique state, to be understood within its own terms, or is it a random multitude of commonly labelled, culturally dependent phenomena?[1] The former assumption leaves the researcher without tools, whereas the latter robs her or him of a justification for being engaged in the study of ageing in the first place.

5. *How to conduct meaningful communication with people whose language is built upon life-long experience and is imbued with material belonging to other cohorts and generations.*[2] Furthermore, how can an anthropologist expect to cope with universes of relevance completely alien to his or her own experience? If we add to that the government of stereotypical images that rules our view of the old, and the sometimes technical difficulties in making sense of the verbal utterances of elderly people, we might be facing a multifaceted blockage in communication.

6. *Finally, how can a researcher, who is often in mid-career and whose life is presumably not yet coming to a close, "go native" and stand alongside researchees at the brink of the most inexplicable human state—that of death?* This mixed sense of awe and fascination is both a drive and a deterrent for anthropologists who consider the world of the aged as a viable field of study. This draws them near the limits of their understanding of the old, but also, first and foremost, of themselves.

If only a few of these caveats are valid, it could be cautiously suggested that the anthropologist of ageing should be looking not only for richer and unbiased material, but mainly for the basic faculties with which the elderly themselves construct and express their world. This implies that elderly persons may develop special cognitive facilities to structure their unique experience. My own various research expeditions into the territories of the aged have undoubtedly endowed me with a respectful recognition of this feat. The premises, nature, and outcomes of the present enquiry could thus be seen as growing from that recognition. Succinctly stated, it claims that the central problem confronted by elderly persons does not arise from issues of role relinquishment, functioning, being social strangers, or the stereotypes and cultural images in which they find themselves entrapped. The key problem, from which the current issues emerge and against which they reverberate, is that aged people exist in a world of disordered time, space, and selfhood. It is a world shot through with paradox. The social construction of the aged as static and immobile stands in absolute contradiction to the personal experience and sensibility of the aged person, who is, in actual fact, undergoing rapid and massive changes. It is this contra-diction that generates a dualistic pattern of behaviour whereby inner con-ceptions, which constitute a type of self-sufficient mythical orientation, no longer inform outer appearances, which are based on common symbolic reference to reality.

If this is the case—and such an assumption is certainly not beyond dispute—then credit must be given to elderly people not only as the pro-ducers of knowledge about themselves, but also as teachers and students of that knowledge. In other words, the role of the anthropologist must be handed over to his "subjects," and instead of the former "going native," a broad leeway should be allocated to the latter to "go anthropologist." As we shall see, our case in point will provide a distinctly clear example of elderly persons producing knowledge about the knowledge of ageing. However, a finely tuned research of any group of elderly people would be able to elicit and elucidate similar findings.

This conclusion can be seen as a logical consequence of the basic dilemma of anthropology with which this chapter began. Not surprisingly, therefore, it echoes parallel proclamations by anthropologists engaged in altogether different fields of interest. Sanjek (1990:412), in an essay de-voted to ethnographic validity, claims that

> In the end, the line between ethnographer and "other" cannot be held. . . . To register fully the ethnographic method's potential, we need radical expansion of ethnography's ranks and the promotion of assistants to "ethnographer," as well as the recognition that ethnographers also may be "assistants" to their informants.

This argument, stemming from the recognition that anthropological dis-course can no longer be confined to its own secret circle whose boundaries reflect those between "civilization" and "natives," finds agreement in Caplan's (1988:17) words that we need to

> think of an ethnography which is not predicated on a dichotomy between self and other . . . the former subjects of objects of study are not only becoming an audience, and a critical one at that, but they are becoming anthropologists themselves.

Examples for such dialectics abound in the short history of anthropol-ogy. The anthropologist John Adair, working at Zuni Pueblo in the late 1940s, had to move to a new residence because the "natives," having read a newspaper article, based on earlier accounts by Cushing, on sacred clowns among the Zuni, became less hospitable. In contrast, 30 years afterwards the Zuni would consult other papers by Cushing in order to better document their ancient rituals. Historically entangled in conflicts of political power and control, the last transformation in the American Indians' complex relationship with anthropologists involves Indian-born trained anthropologists who study American society.

Finally, it is Clifford (1983), whose advocacy of what he calls the polyphonic–interpretative mode focuses on sharing ethnographic authority with the voices of informants (see also Clifford 1986), who also turns to a proposed solution: enlisting the informant as writer and publishing the informants' texts alongside those of the ethnographer. Whereas Clifford's articulation goes hand-in-hand with ours, his ultimate actual solution goes even further. At the conclusion of his essay (1983:146), he cites the example of finally publishing "George Sword, an Oglala warrior and judge," whom ethnographer James Walker had encouraged decades earlier to write his own account of his culture.[3]

The idea of elderly people being their own researchers has indeed been entertained and employed in various settings (e.g., Bass 1987). A case in point, which also carries some interesting consequences for our discussion, is an essay entitled "A Retiree's Perspective on Communication," by Professor Leo Haak and included in Oyer and Oyer's (1976) *Ageing and Communication*. The authors present this chapter, in their introduction, by connecting its significance with the contributor's age: Haak is also well aware of that advocacy and opens by pointing out that "this chapter may be unconventional . . . because it is written by 'one of them'—a retiree" (1976:17). The need for these introductory proclamations is realized once we encounter the original crux of the chapter, the unique observation that sets it apart from the rest: "It is fairly easy to talk about aging and older people," writes Haak (1976:19), "but it is more difficult to talk about aging with older people. Communication is often stopped before it begins." This acute observation of the profound breach in communication between old and non-old can thus be seen as a starting-point for our own enquiry, and one with which chapter 3 is directly concerned.

A twofold objective, therefore, is aimed at. It is imperative that a systematic account of self-knowledge should be obtained from the elderly themselves; and it should be important to have this knowledge reflected upon by those producing it. It is hence assumed—as ethnomethodology would have it—that people's accounts are produced in a meaningful manner and reflect social practices; it is therefore the undertaking of the observer to decipher these accounts and to present a formal analysis of their codex or indexicality.

Another advantage of resorting to ethnomethodological guidance is the useful distinction made by A. Cicourel (1972) between "basic rules" and "surface rules," the former being the mentally entrenched fundamentals of reasoning and construction that underlie accounts, and the latter being the fleeting, ever-changing, culturally laden patterns of social representations provided in these accounts.[4] Difficult as it might be, I am seeking the dividing-line between the two sets and the infra-structure consisting of such basic rules. This distinction between "basic" and "surface" was further developed by B. Bernstein (1977, 1990), who recently referred to it as "recognition rules" and "realization rules"—recognizing the speciality of a context and realizing the specialized communicative means (i.e. restricted or elaborated code) befitting it (Bernstein 1990:15, 98). The codes regulated by the context thus also serve to sustain it. We come back to this crucial point in the final discussion, focusing on the ways by which three possible modes of articulation (defined in chapter 3) act as a context-structuring devices.

Having said what my methodology is about, let me state in brief what it does not pretend to accomplish. I am not interested here with the analysis of singular words or phrases in the methods refined by philosophers of ordinary language, such as J. Austin (1962) and J. Searle (1979). Nor are there any tedious analyses of turn-taking, phonological markers, or diglossia, or descriptions of fricatives, glottalization, anaphoras, or endophoras. All of these are highly technical and of interest only to the dedicated specialist. Instead, the purpose of this work is to focus on the overall role played by language in the life and outlook of elderly speakers. Ethnomethodology and ordinary language philosophy here join forces, as both are interested in meaning by context and by use, where "we ought to look at what happens as a 'proto-phenomenon', asking 'what kind of language game is played here.' . . . For if language is to be a means of communication, there must be agreement not only in definitions, but also (queer as this may sound) in judgements" (Wittgenstein 1953:654).

Deprived of cultural templates and social reinforcement, elderly people face up to the stark foundation of human life. Survival under such conditions is not just a matter of resources, care, or even empathy. It is primarily the unaided search for a new sense of existence. This search is, indeed, the set target of this book, and its three components—discourse, text, and context—constitute the argument and layout of its chapters.

Chapter 1 outlined the discourse of andragogy and discussed the unique properties of the research arena—the U3A—as a safe haven for the third age. Chapter 2 is set to explore the discourse pertaining to the language(s) of the elderly—in terms both of the social construction of this age-group and of this book's quest for the essential propositions of life-span communication in general. It should be noted here that the choice of subjects whose mental competence and communicative potential were beyond dispute was not incidental. It is a matter of supreme importance for the sake of the argument and its rationale to stress that we are dealing here with behavioural products originated by people who are mentally sound and socially alert. The exigency of making prior provision to avert such possible reservations is amplified by the growing trend towards the medicalization of old age[5] and hence the plausible exclusion of any pattern of behaviour reproduced by the elderly from the world of the "normal." It is also noteworthy to indicate that the same methodological consideration applies to the researchee's economic conditions, which could not possibly account for behaviour driven by deprivation. The population involved in this study bears such social trappings of socially approved normalcy that discreditation on those grounds is rendered inconceivable.[6]

The four chapters of part II introduce the reader to the textual world of the research. Produced in the course of group discussions, the verbal texture of knowledge obtained reflects an exchange of opinions. The order of those four chapters allows a systematic overview of the deconstructive[7] character of the debates. Chapter 3 draws on the principles of and justification for deconstructing world-views, while chapters 4, 5, and 6 describe the dismantling of social time, social space, and cultural meaning, respectively.

The four chapters of part III are devoted to an account of the behaviour pursuant to the textually manifested rules. It is only here that I first discuss the particular context of activities in the U3A, for it is this book's underlying argument that these activities cannot be genuinely understood unless the epistemological coordinates of their description are properly laid out in advance, and the already existing curtain of the social discourse on the aged is set aside. Three modes of behaviour in terms of time, space, and reason are then described, along with their corresponding sets of modes of articulation designed to reconstitute time, redelineate space, and maintain an autonomous mastery of portions of reality. These are all instruments in the experiment of testing out articulations and meanings of, as well as mechanisms of coping with, old age.

CHAPTER **3**

Audibility:
A Question of Language

The anthropologist's quest for an adequate language can be compared to that of the U3A people, who were experimenting with different modes of articulation that can relate to past experience and anticipate the future. In order to understand the possibilities and problems involved in such an experiment, this chapter proposes an analytic framework for discussing modes of articulation in relation to age categories. I use the somewhat vague term "modes of articulation" to denote (linguistic) performance as well as (cognitive) competence. Such modes inevitably reflect the duality of personhood and society, of authenticity (if there is any), and normative control. The various ways in which society mutes the voice of the aged must be exposed before examining the counter-ways in which this voice is articulated.

Knowledge about the old is usually produced and disseminated by the non-old. As such, it reflects the enigmatic qualities ascribed to ageing and the aged by the non-aged. The trope of the incomprehensible old is not necessarily occupied by the "confused," bed-ridden, and house-bound category of elderly people. It involves all individuals who, by mere virtue of their chronological age, are discarded into the untouchable caste of the doomed. It is, indeed, the unavoidable but nevertheless avoided association between death and the old that endows the latter with taboo-like attributes. The category of the old as a culturally constructed whole spells a symbolic space where the standards of everyday communication and appreciation do not apply. It is, however, also evident that with advanced age, decrepitude, and growing dependency, the congruence between that culturally constructed symbolic space and the human objects occupying it becomes increasingly consistent.

Society mutes the voice of the old by applying various methods of screening, so that what is heard on the receiving end of that distorted line is inevitably selective to befit social interests and expectations. The portrayal of aged persons as victims of crime, social abuse, poverty, family neglect, and medical maltreatment articulates a common language about ageing that attests only to its medicalization, victimization, marginalization, infantilization, and stigmatization. In a word, ageing is made a social problem.

Examples of the subjugating discourse of old age are abundant. Presumptions as to the pathological nature of ageing, for example, play a major part in medicalizing almost all forms of communication by the old. Since diagnosis of geriatrically related syndromes is not always decidedly clinched and hence rests within a grey scientific area,[1] the range of superimposed medical labels pertaining to ageing is almost infinite. More often than not, a common interest of both physician and custodians formulates the condition of the old in medically intelligible terms so that supervisory measures can be applied. The old person is expected to comply with a set of tests purporting to evaluate her or his cognitive capacities and designed to establish adaptive properties. Failure to meet such standards by appropriately demonstrated aptitudes would result in the classification of the subject as incompetent and thus in need of care and attention. In other words, the old is deemed disoriented, maladjusted, and incoherent, unless proven otherwise. Consequently, any information produced by an old person about herself or himself and the world, unless congruous with the construction of reality of the non-old, is liable to be discredited. Hence, repetitious locutions uttered by elderly persons, adherence to maxims and aphorisms, a-chronological accounts of life histories, inconsistent speech-acts, profuse recourse to reminiscences, or, alternatively, dead silence—all serve as testimonies to "garbled talk," "disorientation," and "senility." It has been shown that supposedly neutral speech cues, such as a slow rate of speech, bad pronunciation, and other age markers, lead hearers to draw downgrading stereotypical inferences such as "doddery," "vague," "frail," and "upset" (Giles, Williams, & Coupland 1990:111).

The reduction of the old into corporeal attributes not only restricts the language about ageing to physiological determinants, but also introduces a split within the Western cultural "paradigm" of the indivisibility of body and soul. It confines the old to a category of social treatment such as medicine or the social welfare system, where bodies are separated from selves. It is intriguing to observe that protest against the social abandonment of the old often invokes the "invisibility" (e.g. Myerhoff 1984) of the elderly as an insignia of such avoidance. However, the sad condition of the elderly put under the social gaze is one of over-visibility, as the old in fact exist only as long as they are being seen (*être vue*, in the words of Sartre). Indeed, it is the separation of bodies from selves that makes the aged only too visible. The old, the patient, and the defendant all share the over-visibility of a subject objectified and a person-cum-persona. Still, it is visibility rather than audibility that becomes a banner against discrimination and inadvertently reinforces it.

Socio-cultural research into the experience of ageing has formulated its frustrations by contriving concepts and theories that attest to the aborted attempt to make sense of old age in conventional socio-anthropological terms. In fact, the very phrasing of these concepts is a self-evident admission to this failure; they all revert to nomenclature and hypotheses, and this negates rather than explains the subject at hand. Thus the elderly have been sociologically declared to be "roleless,"[2] "deculturized,"[3] in a state of "no exit"[4] or of "anomie,"[5] "disengaged,"[6] and symbolically "invisible".[7] To rectify this conceptual myopia, a multitude of alternative constructs have been proposed, none of which stems from the self-expressed world of the aged; all draw on social models for the aged and, indeed, for the non-aged. Hence activity (see Havighurst 1954, 1963, 1975; Lemon et al. 1972), continuity,[8] life-span development[9] and cultural themes[10] were enlisted as key explanatory forms. The assumption that old age is a mere sociological extension of the other ages of man reigns supreme in the various modes and models of understanding ageing, while elderly people are denied the otherwise common intellectual right to present their own world-view to the middle-aged scientific community studying them.

"Old age" is represented by and to middle-aged society through the so-called "mask of ageing." The subject of ageing is masked, concealed behind specular stereotypes, objectified through medical and gerontological discourses. The public self-presentation of the elderly, often made to conform to its social image, further re-enforces this image. Hepworth and Featherstone's (1991) important concept of the "mask of ageing" recapitulates much conceptualization already suggested in the sociology of ageing (e.g., Hazan 1994; Gubrium 1994). It proposes that the image of the elderly is part of the scopic regimes of modernity whose other inmates are the sick (most recently and blatantly, the HIV/AIDS patient), the insane, the primitive, and, ultimately, the "other" in all of its embodiments. The sociology of ageing, itself a powerful image-maker, is also part of this scopic regime. It is part of the ocular centrism of contemporary society and sociology, which gives prominence to the image and privileges sight over sound (Jay 1988a, 1988b). The ocularcentric gaze of the sociology of ageing, even when self-reflexive, has tended to emphasize the visual: either the hyper-visibility of the "mask" of ageing or its complementary opposite, namely the social "invisibility" of the elderly (e.g., Eckert 1980; Myerhoff 1982; Unruh 1983).

Masking is often a repressive act. Woodward (1991), for example, argues that the repression of ageing is connected to the visible oppression of old people in our society. Following Germaine Greer's contention, in her recent book *The Change,* that old age generates angst, Woodward proposes that ageing is not only seen as a general catastrophe but is also particularly associated with women, reflecting a Western "gerontophobia" from the ageing body, regarded as bad, and split off from the youthful body, which is regarded as good. While the image of the elderly should be deconstructed and unmasked, the attempt may prove self-defeating. Invoking both hyper-visibility and invisibility as a banner against ageism may be self-subversive, as it carries the risk of inadvertently strengthening that which it seeks to criticize. Conjuring up images, even in a critical manner, already reproduces them. To avoid this double bind, this book suggests another metaphorical venue into the world of old age: not (in)visibility, but (in)audibility. We make here an attempt to lend an ear to the voices of the old rather than placing them under the sociological gaze. This is intended as a possible means of evading the tyranny of the mirror-hall of images, of what Jay (1988a) calls the scopic regime of perspectival order.

Oral languages, indeed discursive practices at large, have, of course, their own system of normative controls—the "prison house of language" which is articulated here through the metaphors of "muting" and "dubbing." However, there is yet a more significant reason for our preference of the oral over the visual. The quest of the elderly (or of their advocates') to eliminate at least some of the burden of representation and find ways of counter-expression can be better realized through speech rather than vision. The "invisible social worlds" (Unruh 1983) of the elderly are thus often based on ritualized forms of talk (e.g., story-telling, discussion groups, proverbs etc., all to be later explored). It is no surprise that, to Richard the II, it is "the tongues of dying men"—rather than their looks— that command attention "like deep harmony." It is also not surprising that the alternative, namely the loss of aura, is strongly related to the loss of orality, as Walter Benjamin insists in his own critique of visual society, the society of spectacle(s) (see Carey 1987). The question of why elderly people are so pre-occupied with the oral, and the various forms this pre-occupation takes in the postmodern, could arguably define a new agenda for a sociology of ageing that is sensitive to its narrative moment (Maines 1993).

AUDITING THE LIFE SPAN:
THE DISCURSIVE FORMULATION OF AGE GROUPS

Age groups are constituted through cultural anticipations, echoed in the various metaphors related in each and every society to the "seasons of man's life" (Levinson et al. 1978). Such a social span of control demands different discursive frames of reference for "hearing," "discussing," "explaining," and ultimately "understanding" the various age groups defined. These discourses, in turn, often become part of their subjects' repertoire, internalized into forms of articulation that characterize the symbolic exchange practised among members of the age group and between this group and others.

Using old age as a reference-point, this chapter critically reconsiders these themes. "Old age," we argue, is a symbolic category defined primarily by middle age and mainly through two discursive systems, or "languages," termed here the "literal" and the "metaphysical".[11] These two discursive formulations of "old age" imply two socially reified views of the life-span, respectively: the "life cycle" and the "life course." The "life cycle," the "life course"—and any other institution of the "life span," for that matter—are seen here as being primarily mechanisms of normative control rather than free alternatives open for individual choice. Sociologists have recently suggested that postmodernist trends are loosening the normative control over age boundaries and age identities (e.g., Giddens 1991; Featherstone & Hepworth 1990, 1991; Coupland & Nussbaum 1993). Postmodern changes, it has been argued, are leading to both a greater differentiation of age grades (i.e., adolescence, college years, early adulthood, middle age, and the third age), as well as to some blurring of previously age-associated experiences and characteristics (Meyerowitz 1984). These assumed trends have caused Featherstone and Hepworth (1991) to coin the term "uni-age style." The multi-faceted postmodern reality of cycles, courses, new-age categories, and "uni-age style" are considered here, in contrast, from its "dark" side: not as the result of some "project of modernity" reflecting the (capitalist) dream-come-true of progress, plenitude, and equal opportunities, but, rather, as the product of the invisible yet ever-growing disciplinary and normalizing discourse of postmodernity. The normative control exerted by the discourse of ageing is as profound as it is dispersed. This is congruent with the character of postmodern authority structures, which "cannot demand obedience by invoking explicitly its putative right to command. Commanding as such has been discredited as oppression. . . . An effective authority must not appear to be an authority—but a helpful hand, a well-wisher, a friend" (Bauman 1992:196). In a word, it is the structures of authority that have become largely invisible, while the elderly remain to a large extent over-visible, yet inaudible. We do not argue that this interpretation is exclusive to old age. It is offered here as one complementary reading of the social reality of age-related discourses. "Ultimately, the life span can be understood as a panorama of cultures. What we are witnessing here," observes Friedman (1987:35), "is the collapse of an authority structure, one that defines the superiority of adulthood, of rational discourse, of standard linguistic usage." While this interpretation may very well apply to some of post-modern disconnected life worlds, we wish to add to it yet another perspective. Observing "old age," this chapter examines how it is social identity that is collapsing while the superiority of adulthood—as compared to both "childhood" and "old age"—is rationalized and legitimized.

Let me first discuss how middle age uses literal language in order to define old age. It has already been pointed out at the beginning of this chapter that mass media, welfare criteria, and social stereotypes provide programmes of talking about the old, which are further validated by selectively induced expressions uttered by elderly people. Pre-assumptions as to the pathological nature of ageing, for example, play a major part in medicalizing almost all forms of communication by the old. The old person is further expected to comply with a set of tests purporting to question and evaluate her or his cognitive capacities and designed to establish adaptive properties and measure "life satisfaction" (Gubrium & Lynott 1983).

Old age and childhood are prescribed with structurally similar social positions through the use of literal language. In childhood, this is the language of socialization,[12] which only gradually develops into non-literal forms such as irony and metaphor (Winner 1990; see also Astington 1991; Trevarthen & Logotheri 1989). Story-telling whose moral is emphasized is presumably shared by both children and the elderly. As in the case of nursery rhymes, folk-tales, and legends, the stories of the elderly are viewed as "plotted prose with an explicit moral" (Mergler & Goldstein 1983:86), based on common narratives, idioms, and proverbial vocabularies (Koch 1977; Blythes 1979; Coupland & Coupland 1991; Myerhoff 1978a). The "deculturated" (Anderson 1972) discourse of "life-reviewing" and "reminiscence" of the elderly can be regarded as symmetrical with the socializing discourse of nursery tales and "secret-sharing" in childhood (Katriel 1991). Both share a master narrative based on literality, metonymy,[13] self-referentiality, and myth-like qualities (see also Searle 1979, on literal meaning). Some psycho-linguists even ventured to state that this "literal talk" is a result of deficiencies in working memory and linguistic competence (Kemper 1988). The literal, found both in childhood and in later life, thus presents itself as an extremity—as either a point of entrance, a marker of socialization, or as a point of departure, a sign of deculturation.

In contrast to youth and old age, middle age (as conceived of and constituted by its own occupants) dictates other constraints and social prescriptions. The ideal type of mid-life is concerned with effectiveness and objective information, the aligning of desires and capabilities in everyday domains such as work, love, and family life (Smelser & Erikson 1980; Hepworth & Featherstone 1982). This demands a pragmatic disposition and an outward-oriented, objective frame of reference, which is furthermore capable of metaphorically—that is, non-literally—interconnecting the various life-worlds (e.g., professional, familial, consumerist, political, etc.) of middle age. Such a pragmatic, metaphorical, "better-equipped" disposition, once defined, can be used to separate and distinguish middle age both from childhood and from old age.

In addition to the more commonly used practices of literal discourse that account for both childhood and old age as well as making both categories accountable to the social order of middle age, as discussed earlier, there is yet another language that is part of the "discourse of ageing." This language is by and large reserved for designating old age. It is a metaphysical language, which has become the interpreting framework for discussing and authorizing the so-called "ageing self." "Ego integrity" (Erikson 1982) and "the ageless self" (Kaufmann 1986) are two such idealized, metaphysical cultural paradigms revealing more of the expectations and fears of middle age than of the actual phenomenology of ageing. The trope of the old is dually occupied by the literally speaking, "confused," bed-ridden, and house-bound elderly, as well as the ageing, metaphysically speaking "blind prophet."[14] It is dually constituted by the archetypal "scheming hag" as well as by the literal stereotype of the "dear old thing" (Cool & McCabe 1983).

Metaphysical interpretation is often evoked by proponents of "old-age style." Woodward (1980), for example, who studied the late poems of Eliot, Pound, Stevens, and Williams, argues that ageing puts the poet in a position to see "the whole of the system." In Cohen-Shalev's (1992:297) account of the late style of novelists as well as artists, it is defined as "a tendency to strip down artifice." "The relative lack of distinction between fact and fantasy, autobiography and invention, prose and poetry," he claims, "does not result in a harmonious resolution of these opposites, but, rather, in a coexistence that seems to transcend logical thought categories." Viewing the elderly as incorporating the ability to "see the whole system" and "to strip down (social) artifice" is part of the metaphysical discourse of marginalization, which endows ageing not only with the prescriptions of liminality but also with the powers of estrangement. It is the unavoidable, but nevertheless avoided association between death and the old that endows the latter with such a metaphysical language. "O, but they say the tongues of dying men," laments Richard the II, "enforce attention like deep harmony."

The three different age-related languages (literal, metaphysical, non-literal) can now be superimposed onto one's path of life.[15] The dominant model found in the final stage of life in effect defines it as either a course or a cycle:

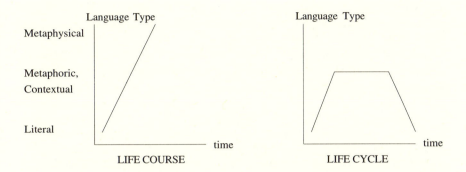

The second chart—that of the "life cycle"—is very similar to another graph, found in Turner (1987:123), which represents childhood and old age as homologous in terms of social liminality and disengagement, or what Turner calls lack of reciprocity, which is (according to him) the basis for social prestige.

Turner's narrative, therefore, belongs to the "life-cycle" type, in which youth and old age are symmetrically constructed through the literal language. "Because the child and the elderly share a number of common social characteristics (such as the absence of work and social responsibilities, or "roles") they are often described in the same pejorative and stigmatizing fashion" (Turner 1987:123). Childhood and old age, socialization and deculturation, irresponsibility and disengagement, are all the outcomes of social regulation. The dominance of literal language in those two extremes of the life cycle—childhood and old age—can also be seen as such an outcome. It is more of a socially prescribed language than an inherent part of these groups. "To speak literally" can serve as a normative control mechanism in its own right, mainly as it obliterates the need to decode the speaker's idiosyncratic, non-literal intentions. Literal language is, therefore, the key to what Hockey and James (1993) call, in a very similar manner, the discourse of infantilization:

> the cultural pervasiveness of metaphors of childhood within the discourses surrounding ageing and dependency . . . has become "naturalized." It is seen as somehow inevitable, as the way things are. Through this culturally constructed model of dependency, many of those in old age and others who are infantilized—the chronically sick or disabled, for example—may be made to take a conceptual position alongside children on the margins of society. [1993:13]

To what extent does that "Episteme" become internalized by those subjected to it,[16] to what extent does it become their frame of mind? These questions are further referred to in the discussion.

The metaphysical language is, in purpose, no different from the literal. Through it, the nomadic ageing self in late modern society is masked, muted, dubbed, and ultimately defined as the metaphysical object of "pilgrimage through life." Giddens (1991) argues that the postmodern blurring of age structure is closely linked to the rejection of the pre-destination narrative of identity that long dominated Western thought. In his words (1991:14),

> Self-identity for us [in the late modern age] forms a trajectory across different institutional settings of modernity over the duree of what used to be called the "life cycle," a term which applies more accurately to non-modern contexts than to modern ones. Modernity is a post-traditional order, in which the question, "How shall I live?" has to be answered in day-to-day decisions about how to behave, what to wear and what to eat—and many other things—as well as interpreted within the temporal unfolding of self-identity.

Bauman (1992) distinguishes between two symbolic types of "identity seekers": the postmodernist nomads and the Protestant (modernist) "pilgrims through life." The former wander between unconnected places; they have no pre-set itinerary, and hence only momentary identities, identities "for today," until-further-notice identities. Pre-destination has been replaced, in their case, with uncertainty. The "pilgrims" have their destination pre-selected (by religion, society, gender, class, origin, etc.), and they guide their life according to a "life-project," crystallizing a single core-identity throughout this "path of life." The "nomads" can be said to move further in the life span, while "pilgrims" either "progress" in the "life course" or continue along the "life cycle." Western adult society, postmodernist and all, by and large still considers its elderly according to the second narrative—that of pilgrimage.

"Literal" and "metaphysical," in the case of the elderly, are two sides of the same coin—in other words, a matter of interpretation. "The language of the elder is perhaps simply all language made plain," argue Mergler and Schleifer (1985); but "speaking plainly" can be both literal and metaphysical. This ambiguity is echoed in a late poem of Stevens (1954:510), which states that "With every visible thing enlarged and yet No more than a bed, a chair and moving nuns."

There is an ambiguity inherent in the ageing situation of simultaneously possessing a sense of self and one of otherness about oneself, a situation emanating from the split between the "I" and the "me" (see next section). Furthermore, it is because of this complete split in the life-worlds of the elderly that metaphor—being a symbolic vehicle designed to connect different worlds by means of some analogy (Davidson 1979)—becomes impossible. It is only within such a split, for example, that "habit" can be understood as both a (literal) weary repetition and a (metaphysical) crystallization in which "the past is brought to life again, the future anticipated" (de Beauvoir 1975:696). Literal or metaphysical interpretation, in the case of both childhood and old age, does not hinge on the speaker's own intention, but, rather, on some collective knowledge, a socially shared record of images and stereotypes. This disciplinary convention is crucial in the case of the old. Where autobiography is too idiosyncratic and relationships are built on non-reactive networks (i.e., "social worlds," see Unruh 1983), non-literal personal meaning is hardly communicable. The literal and the metaphysical, therefore, befit the discourse of ageing as both a social measure of normative control and a form of speech. It enables one to understand one's words without having to decipher, in the process, one's world. The old speaker's world is hence too often obscured by the discourse of ageing.

The structural comparison drawn between childhood and old age points to yet another aspect of the specific age group under study. It should be remembered that the members of the U3A distinctly referred to themselves as belonging not to the category of "old age" but to a category they called the "third age." They even created an academic organization to stand as evidence to the existence of such a "third age." This category is defined as preceding "old age," but still as different from it. One member of the discussion group reflected on the subject by saying,"I wonder whether it has occurred to anybody else here that we are a very curious group, but then again we are not really old. We may say that we are ante-aged."

But what is "ante-aged"? It was, in the eyes of members, a social buffer zone between past upward careers and social integration on the one hand, and prospects of disengagement and deterioration on the other. Following the "life-cycle" symmetry, I argue that the age group that is symmetrical to the third age is, in effect, adolescence. The third age, one might say, is the "adolescence of old age." "Ante-aged" is symmetrical with "post-childhood" (note that the life-cycle symmetry is of a reverse type—which is one of the reflections of the socially prescribed character of this paradigm). Moreover, third age and adolescence share a number of social characteristics. First and foremost, they are considered as betwixt and between—already out of their former age category, but still not part of the next. This sense of "half-baked" categories depicts them as being caught up in ambiguity and crisis. Most significantly, these characteristics lend these age categories a social license to experiment—experiment with values, norms, social conduct, and personal behaviour. I believe that their (perhaps unconscious) identification with those characteristics underpinned the creation of a "third age" by the members of the U3A, and indeed by ageing people involved in such a movement all around the world. It was this sense of ambiguity and crisis, as well as the urge to experiment with new frames of mind, that undermined the whole project of the third age. It remains, of course, to be seen whether and how these sweeping assumptions are reflected in the texts produced by the elderly people.

Literal, metaphysical, and non-literal have become, in the case of the U3A members, incongruent and mutually exclusive. Whereas usually these languages are interwoven and mixed, in the discussion group (as in old age generally) they have become differentiated. The elderly in the discussion group experimented with these modes of thought and dispersed them, as we shall further see, into three distinct "softwares." The very quest for things-in-themselves and first principles, in which the U3A members were engaged, demanded the practice of a language of essentials, which was deliberately divorced by these members from their other, practical languages. This division entailed a unique dismissal of meta-communication, which expressed itself—among other things—in the conspicuous refraining from dramatic activities or any role-playing. This lack of meta-communication, and the alternative ways devised to handle the growing gap between practical and essential language in old age, are addressed in the concluding part of the book. Other questions regard the means employed by U3A members in order to transform the chronological time of inevitable decline into a new, recursive, and non-linear temporality. This transformation is also considered in conjunction with the substitution of former careers, roles, and statuses by an autonomous and egalitarian social sanctuary of one's peers.

PART II

TEXT:
SOUNDINGS OF
THE CODE OF AGEING

All that philosophy can teach,
The lore of jurist and of leech,
I've master'd, ah! and sweated through
Theology's dead deserts, too (—)

If I cannot escape the bitter woe
Of babbling of things that I do not know,
And get to the root of those secret powers,
Which hold together this world of ours,
The sources and centres of force explore,
And chaffer and dabble in words no more.

[Faust: opening monologue]

CHAPTER 4

Terms of Reference:
"Taking It from First Principles"

In chapter 3 I argued that a new age category called the "third age" was constructed by members of the U3A in order to serve as a buffer zone between maturity and elderliness. Furthermore, this buffer zone, or "limbo state" (Hazan 1980) lent members—in a manner somewhat parallel to that of adolescence—a social license for experimentation. This experimentation reflects a unique frame of mind that accompanied involvement in the third age. It was a disposition to contemplate and review life in general and taken-for-granted assumptions in particular. In effect, the meetings became a laboratory for reformulating knowledge about the world, and they did this by dismantling this knowledge through its "modes of articulation"—the three "languages" discussed in chapter 3. How this was done is the subject of the following four chapters, collectively entitled "soundings of the code of ageing." Why, or for what purpose, it was done is discussed in part III, entitled "testing out for ageing."

Immediately upon our first meeting, participants declared that they were not interested in talking about "things," nor were they concerned with "learning." Rather, they insisted on having a free-floating discussion about "us," meaning the people present in the room—or, as it turned out to be, "humanity" as a whole.

The overt aversion to any form of formal learning was explained as an objection to being "brainwashed" or even "taught to." Later on it emerged that more deeply rooted reasons stood at the basis of this reluctance. The negative rhetoric of learning was so significant to them as to suggest that the word "university" should be removed from the title of the organization to which they belonged and that the term "club" ought to replace it.

Learning was a disdained concept, for it implied the introduction of "arbitrary assumptions as if they were unquestionable truths." Arbitrariness was deemed to entail the imposition of somebody else's will without justification or reasoning. But, according to the teachings of the group, "everything must have reason," and hence "we must get to the root of things in order to understand them." However, this idealistic quest for the foundation of truth was difficult to reconcile with the way of life these people had led in pursuit of professional careers, financial security, and social status. They resolved this contradiction through a declared separation between the two pursuits—the ideal and the pragmatic. None of them hesitated to admit to succumbing to the rules of thumb of practical reasoning in conducting everyday living.[1] The pragmatic approach advocated by members was indeed a broad and sweeping perspective embracing knowledge of cultural values and social norms as "tools for survival." It is interesting to note already at this stage something that was to increase in importance as the course of the presentation developed—that is, the abandonment of the language of culture, with its symbols, myths, and rituals, as an essential drive and fundamental code in one's life. The notion that culture is merely a practical device suggests that there must be a domain of experience or rules beyond it.

That domain, to be located in the general principles of human conduct and adherence to social conventions, is only justifiable as a matter of mutual expedience: "I respect other people's views and opinions because I want them to respect mine. I would even respect the abhorrent idea of apartheid in South Africa." The conviction underlying such assertions is that views, opinions, "proper" behaviour, and cultural performance are not necessarily informed by the general principles of existence and hence ideals or, rather, ideas (in the Platonic sense) and the exigencies of survival do not meet and can be kept separate.

Having established this split, the group devoted a great many of its debates to deliberations over the question of the nature and the presence of those basic principles. A necessary step in that direction was to have some mistakenly conceived principles exposed. Such disguises were unmasked through persistent reiteration of the rebuttal of learning.

Being so familiar with "high language" and with academic "hifaluting" jargon in particular, members did not find it too difficult to denote the kind of terminology whose obliteration they sought. Thus they stated their objection to "semantic interpretation of words" and to the "excessive use and misuse of abstract concepts in our society." This was followed by elaborations of the areas where concepts reign supreme and ought therefore to be ignored. The argument developed among members maintained that concepts and symbols are created and cultivated to sustain artificial, arbitrary boundaries between disciplines of knowledge. Knowledge is indivisible, and splitting it into "fields" and "areas" of specialization only muffles its essential voice.

Essence was, indeed, the key term employed by members. While rejecting any academically oriented discourse, they declared their commitment to striving towards the essence of things and "taking everything from first principles." This phrase was abundantly repeated and related to throughout the discussions.

The implications of this search for "first principles" as seen by members extended from refusing to engage in "a rigorous but futile academic discussion" to the demand that the divides between disciplines of knowledge should be broken down. This was accompanied by an emphatic denial of any possible contribution of formal theory or other conceptual frameworks to the understanding of the "essence." The reason for this critical view of theoretical thinking was particularly enlightening since it was advanced by people whose professional lives had been guided by theoretical models and academic considerations. They explained that their life-long experience had taught them that nothing is static and constant and that everything flows and changes. Theories and concepts, therefore, are man-made means of transfixing reality, where reality itself is all about dynamics and transformation. Models of life were conceived to be feigned images of experience and as such had to be avoided. It should be noted, however, that what might be construed as a contradiction in terms—that is, between the pledge to lability and the commitment to the discovery of essence—is a false incongruity, since, as was previously demonstrated, perennial ideals do not inform ephemeral practicalities. Far from being a far-fetched interpretation to an apparent misnomer, this explanation is supported by one of the members to the effect that "We try to get to the heart of the matter, even though, and maybe because, we are so very practical." This self-observation also accounted for the permission granted to the anthropologist to attend meetings. Anthropology, unlike other sciences, seemed to members a rare academic haven of non-conceptual thinking. Anthropologists won their approval due to their assumed preoccupation with "reality itself" and because of their endeavour "to question the taken for granted in everyday life." Some members even offered first-hand evidence to validate this portrayal of anthropology by dwelling on their own academic training, recalling courses in social anthropology taken in the 1920s or 1930s.

The gracious inclusion of anthropology into the cannon of legitimate issues under discussion was but one example of the mental agility articulated by members. Being highly conscious of this acquired competence, they formulated it as an unavoidable consequence of the freedom of choice they were expected and accustomed to exercise throughout their professional life. Being doctors, engineers, businessmen, and teachers they had all occupied positions of power and, therefore, decision making, and this provided the rationale for the extreme verbal alacrity and the open-ended span of choices that they exhibited. As one of the members put it: "We are neither determinists nor fatalists, we are realistic"—and, for them, change and unpredictability were the mutable cornerstones of this state.

The following exchange—transcribed from a tape recording—was stimulated by a discussion about the interchangeability of technologies and the fluidity of corresponding scientific concepts. Pragmatism is again the order of the day, while the ability to accommodate oneself to the ever-changing world is one of the components constituting the "essence of humanity":

— "Now—it's more difficult to think in terms of a human being who has been brought up with a set of concepts—some of them very deeply embedded—and it's not easy to think that if you have changed, these would be exchanged for other ones. But I think what is universal is that these things are evolved in order, initially, just to survive. Now, the first proof of the pudding is that you do survive. Obviously, it's not just survival in a physical sense, but being able to both work with others and to derive some satisfaction in your life, and so on. Those are the tests of whether your particular constructs are right or wrong. The first thing that hits you, no doubt, is that you started with a set of concepts and so on, which carry you along during your active life, professional life, and so on. But now, faced with changed circumstances, you start being unhappy in one form or another, eventually suffering other, more severe problems."

— "You'd mean insecurity really?"

— "Insecurity and so on."

— "Which produces unhappiness."

— "Yes, I'm nearly certain about that. And it's then you obviously have to adjust if you want to survive—and sometimes literally survive, because people do die very often early in the day and give up. You have to adjust your concepts, the ones that govern your behaviour and so on, to the new circumstances, and that does require first of all a lot of very hard thinking and, of course, analytical thinking of the highest order about the processes that go on."

— "The thing to remember is that you have to continue to test and continually question things. It's the difference between taking everything for granted and taking certain things for granted—you can't take everything for granted when you get into a situation where somehow your actions do not provide the desired effects, which are some sort of personal satisfaction and so on."

— "Our ability to reflect is not an automatic ability, and this is the thing. It's not an automatic ability. It's an intellectual ability. It's the ability to consider things, to weigh up the factors, and to make a decision."

— "Can I just take it one step further?"

— "Yes."

— "I think it's not just the reflectivity. There's also a sense of creativity in it, something which arises without any input from the outside—you reflect on new ideas, and as a result of that, you can change your view-points."

— "You know, we've all lived for a rather long time, and we can look back to things that have changed in a very radical way in our own lives. For instance, I'm sure we were all brought up on some silly nonsense about 10 little nigger boys when we were small."

— "But it's really an affront to hear someone using the word 'nigger' now."

The paradox of having to dispose of concepts by means of conceptual analysis is not disentangled but is recognized and related to, as one of the members put it: "the biggest obstacle—the mind." Further elaboration of this struggle between the intellect and the world of ideals is offered in the following:

— "I have in our family two dyslexics, one of whom can read, but who doesn't take to books at all, and the other one who hasn't taken to them yet. He reads the sports page in the newspapers and virtually nothing else."

— "I think you shouldn't use the word 'dyslexic'."

— "All right. But it refers to specific reading disabilities that for the sake of keeping it simple I use the word."

— "That wasn't appropriate."

— "Do you think of the implications?"

— "Well, the question is whether he or she has difficulty in reading."

— "The point I am coming to is that very often such people will get far more out of modern technology—videos, computers, and so forth—by being presented to things with pictures, rather than by some synthetic language."

— "I think that's probably important. But even more important to my mind is the fact—it seems to me we can be in danger of allowing a material attribute to rule our lives. Taking it at its simplest: do we all believe all we read in books?"

— "Likewise, speaking medically, if we have a difficult diagnosis and we get an x-ray which points to something we diagnose, do we diagnose it on our clinical acumen or on the x-ray?"

— "Also, I'm not sure that the *Encyclopaedia Britannica* isn't yet called the 'Encyclopaedia Chicago.'"

— "No."

— "It's a good example, because it's essentially a factual source."

— "I think one changes, and now at various points it gets fixed in law or custom or some other way and you then go on changing, but you are saddled with the awful job of changing the law or changing the method of presenting what is thought to be right. And that's a hindrance. The change goes on all the time. It happens that—there are spectra—I know about a gift of serious nature—was called change in continuity. And I was extremely interested, looking back over 50 years, to see how the actual medical practice and science was continuously changing, and we only adjust to the machinery periodically and with great difficulty. And I think that's what you were talking about in effect."

— "Yes."

— "And the thing starts and—I think that the real weakness is that, the real obstacle is that we keep on forgetting the biggest obstacle is inside our minds. And that the sort of things that you just mentioned now—in other words, that one makes these external changes periodically. What happens in practice surely is that you proceed pragmatically, you see. If you assume, for instance, that you—you know, you've got some sort of a-priori assumptions and you act on those, and you find that you continue to keep on banging your head against the wall because there is no door there, you see, which would be a set of assumptions. Then you start thinking: well, world-picture, paradigm, or whatever doesn't seem to work. And its this kind of signal, I think, that one has to be very sensitive to."

The banging of heads against the wall of concepts becomes unavoidable by virtue of the necessity of resorting to concepts and could be handled by abolishing the link between past experience and current knowledge. Relief from the nexus between the two could be attained by doing away with conceptual mediators that interlink theory with practice:

— "Our world is extremely complicated. We manage with it because we accept a certain number of awful solutions. We can think through any new problem from first principles once and then apply repeatedly. It would be absolutely exhausting and possibly delaying to think through everything from first principles every time, and we generalize this by the printed word. But we are all pretty antique, and we can all think back to the moments when on quite important things we thought again from first principles and changed. Even if it's only the colour of the bedroom curtains, and, I think, really this was what you were raising at the beginning."

— "Yes, that was exactly the point, right. What was involved in that pattern of assumptions, age-group by age-group. And there are certain decisions that in turn induced change, or what were the factors associated with change."

— "There's a different pattern of assumptions, age-group by age-group. And there are children who start with their basis of knowledge correlative on a different frame, years ahead of us, when approaching something new. A classic example was my six-year-old grandson, saying to my wife, 'Granny, will you play chess with me?' And the granny said: 'Oh, I can't play chess, Edward,' and he said, 'Of course you can, granny, I taught you last time I was here.'"

— "The fact that our children are more advanced than us in technological terms doesn't mean that it has any bearing on the moral order or the generations."

— "It's the handling of information."

— "Yes, exactly."

— "Yes, but even though, you do raise something interesting. I wasn't thinking so much of moral order. You see, we've been concentrating on the cognitive, the reasoning and rational processes. But, of course, equally important to us are the emotive processes, the feeling, and what you're thinking on in aesthetic terms, for instance, and so on. Now, those are based on different—you know—different premises in a different way. And maybe children, through concentrating on a particular thing at that time, are losing out on the other one, which they have tried. And, of course, you know that our life is extremely artificial nowadays compared to that of our childhood, when we spent a good deal of time out in the country, and so on."

— "We can't foresee what will happen to the children as they grow up, can you? Your 16-year-old grandson will probably be different from your son."

— "Well, will he be for better or for worse?"

— "Yes."

— "What we can do is to do our best and also to note that when anybody is educated, he has to some extent the duty to go around and pick as many brains as possible. And those brains have a duty to try and see that their pupils are better or at least as good as they are. So it makes sense, the more brains that a pupil can pick, the better he should be in relation to his predecessors. And I trust, now, it doesn't apply just to intellect but also to moral learning."

— "But the real criminal thing would be to ask one to impose our solutions on our children."

— "I think there's little danger of that because the present generation think our solutions are so futile."

— "And, of course, this is all about the old business of people having to rediscover in painful ways the things that otherwise they could pick up."

Children's knowledge of the world and its inculcations is the ultimate challenge to the notion of enduring theory and concepts, and as such it is fully exploited by members. Since the technological supremacy of the young is beyond debate, the only asset the old might possess is their familiarity with the basic principles of life. Knowledge is not omnipotent, nor is it applicable to any experience. Rather, it is subjected to the rules of relativity and ephemerality.

Children are, indeed, a very valid motive for constructing an affixed value system. This was apparently dismissed off-handedly by members who devalued the significance of "feelings" and "love" as transient, and, like any other production of emotional behaviour, as lending themselves to be shaped and moulded by circumstances. At the climax of one discussion, a member even went to the length of saying that "children are not really necessary, but their presence must not be dismissed."

This stance, which repeats itself in numerous ways later on, leaves the gap between word and phenomenon unbridgeable. Words petrify fluid phenomena, and this fundamental breach in the possibility of communication between one's external linguistic expression and his or her internal self is addressed in the following:

— "I like cases to be made fairly specific; my mind boggles when the word 'change' is mentioned. Let's take a couple of examples here, you know. I'm very intrigued by the notion that in fact language almost inhibits, because language is static."

— "Yes, it sort of petrifies the state of affairs. And yet, I think, the language does in fact develop pretty quickly, if you look at what happens, say, in Welsh, how very quickly technological words are incorporated into the language."

— "And the way, in fact, that French has become Americanized because of the social and technological changes. It moves pretty fast, but, as you say, in the mere writing down of a word you are embodying reality, concreting it."

— "It worries me, because it's a question of, when you discuss a problem, whether you discuss the problem itself or whether you avoid discussing the problem by the language you employ—and that in turn depends on what your meta-constructs are. Now, to take the last thing first, it would be no use our discussing the issue and phenomenon of the computer here; and it's no use our complaining that those who are knowledgeable use some different language about it. If you have a new concept arising, you have to invent one, and that would be to those who have not yet taken part in this development a strange word. I ask you all to recall one of the famous paradoxes which occurred in Greek law, and that is the famous chase of the tortoise and the hare. Now, this is, as you know, not just a funny story, but it was a real problem which occupied philosophers for a long time. Now, it existed as a problem purely and simply because they didn't have the intellectual tools to tackle problems of that kind. It is a non-problem. You see, once you can enter modern concepts of rate of change, pace, and so on, then the problem of the tortoise and the hare doesn't exist."

— "Now, you see, the reason why the philosophers were worried was because it was patently opposite to common terms and common action."

— "But of course."

— "And yet they held views the most rigorous of which was about their disposal of the problem, which in turn was based on a developed framework of thinking. The thing is, that talking about the language as a sort of enduring and concrete change and so on is just as nonsensical to me as the question of why the hare cannot catch up with the tortoise. Because it's by using the inappropriate language that in turn was based on not using the appropriate constructs and concepts. And really this is the thing, and, of course, that doesn't mean that the thing is suddenly crystal simple, because it isn't."

— "Yes, sure."

— "Unless one uses clear and appropriate language of a sort, then I don't think one can get to another problem. I'd like to tell you a story. H. W. B. Joseph of New College was one of the foremost logicians in Europe 50–60 years ago, and he was my moral tutor, poor chap. And once I went to lunch at his house, and we were playing one of those ridiculous games around the table, and asking silly questions. And somebody postulated that if an express train started from London to Carlisle at X hours and a goods train had started three hours earlier from Carlisle for London, which was further from London when they met? And old Joseph thought for a long time, and then said 'I shall need a piece of paper.' I think something serious comes into this. How crazy can you get?"

— "He was merely ignorant of the subject."

— "Off the hook."

— "It seems to me, and I think probably most people who had the experience of using either foreign languages or, if you like, specialist jargon— will agree that no one language can express all the concepts that we wish to express. I mean, there are many times when one wishes to fall back on medical jargon or on certain German or Latin terms in order to say perhaps more accurately what we find we can't say in common everyday language. Computers are a concept that is really based on machine code which is quite alien to most of us. Because of that, high-level languages have been introduced, Most of it seems to have boiled down to this rather appropriate acronym called BASIC, which I think most people could properly use with a little bit of experience. But BASIC is slow, does not cover many of the concepts of more sophisticated computer programming which most people will want if they are going to use a computer seriously. And also BASIC is not only a language, but it's like any other language which has a large number of dialects, not all of which are comprehensible. So we end up with this—with a slower language, which has now been developed into a fairly compatible dialect. The same thing has happened technologically in computers with the central processing which has been also adopted for many standard processes which is rather 'old hat'. Now, we've seen all this before in the development of railways in Britain, changes that started over a century ago, speaking rather simplistically. Another case of *force majeure*—namely that most people adopted a narrow gauge when a wide gauge would have allowed us to develop much more rapidly and much more effectively. How can we get over these influences in change?"

— "Quite."

— "Yes, but you see, fundamentally, there's no difference in that—between that and, say, the situation that you should suddenly find that the temperature in Cambridge drops a number of degrees as a result of which we have to adapt to it. You start wearing different clothes. But in conceptual terms I don't see any difficulty."

— "Which fills me with joy."

— "You brought the whole issue into relief. Because this is really the crux of the whole matter. Whether there is or there isn't a fundamental change here."

— "You have to change your concepts, you have to change your language. And not your internal language, not only the matter of communicating and so on. But, provided you do that in an orderly fashion, then there is no basic problem. There are certain problems i.e. your decision about whether to buy the *Encyclopaedia Britannica* or to wait for it. It's no different from the problem we used to consider—should we buy a television set or should we rent it? Because the argument was that if in fact that technology was so fluid that no sooner have you bought your television set and spent your capital, it was obsolete. Should you wait for it, and so on? Now, similar problems of this kind mean that we are living through an extremely fast-changing period. This is where, yes, this is I think the fundamental change in paradigm. And I think this is precisely thinking in terms of processes rather than immutable emptiness."

This discourse, like many others, speaks for itself and is yet another testimony to the persistent elimination of various forms of language from the quest for the "essence." Concepts, jargon, nomenclature, classifications, and vocabularies seem to be essentially divergent, but they only differ technically in their capacity to convey messages for the business of living. "Internal language" (whatever that may be), however, remains immutable and responds to the rules of the "essence of things."

Everyday language is then reduced to its functional properties and is relegated to the culturally conditional realm of human behaviour. However, being pragmatically minded as they were, members devoted a great deal of discussion time to elucidating the qualities of language as a channel of communication. Ample scope for a debate along this vein became open to discussants when the issue of "wolf-children" was brought up. It enabled members to embark on the subject of learned behaviour and the adaptive role of concepts. The fact that the "forbidden experiment"—that is, belated acculturation of children raised by animals—invariably produced poor and agonizing results[2] puts a question mark on the view that concepts are merely "things" to be inculcated, used, and abandoned at society's will:

— "Well, language is part of culture. I mean, you can't really separate the two."
— "And language being part of conceptualization."
— "Absolutely. Yes."
— "It's partially cultural because there is also built-in, if you like, a hardwork part of the language and that—you get that crucial development where you actually either form those ways of being able to build up your mental resources or you're not, if you haven't got those basic skills."
— "Yeah."
— "We're talking about some aspects of life which are really human nature. There's plenty of evidence that with the very young, developing child there is a time to do things. You can get this absolutely on certain physical kinds of development. An incompletely deaf child can be taught to use speech and language if it is given auditory training to speak in the ordinary way. If it isn't given it, he never catches up, probably."
— "Oh, yes."
— "And that stuff about maternal deprivation, I would have thought, goes far beyond this sort of wolf-child business. There is ample evidence that a child brought up without real attachment to a mother or a surrogate mother is going to have certain psychological facets of its later character that make it to an extent deprived."
— "Yes."

The pitfall of having to resort to considering the world beyond concepts such as human contact in early upbringing was bypassed by emphasizing the necessary function of concepts as the building blocks of culture and communication, and the imperative of constructing them. Furthermore, concepts were conceived of as concrete objects very much like those they represent:

— "One is aware that once a conceptual unit is put aside, it has no existence of its own. We tend to, of course, verify all our concepts. If I remember that these dollars or whatever are merely a particular calculation for some particular purpose, that wouldn't be so harmful."

— "Yes."

Another challenge to the rule of concept was the much-discussed issue of the rise of fundamentalistic movements around the world. In addition to the utter disgust voiced by members to the phenomenon, they revealed in their response to it the positive role of concepts as the constituents of the knowledge required to dispel the darkness of prejudice:

— "What's the point in discussing them if at any time we have all over the world all sorts of prejudices and things people believe in and so on. And really the more important thing is to start from where we are pretty certain that our knowledge now gives us."

This strong objection to superstition and prejudice was, indeed, shared by all members, but that was only one self-evident facet of their overall attitude towards all matters emotional. This could only be discussed as avoidance reinforced by self-imposed neutrality. Relativistic stances were unequivocally adopted to emphasize their inability or unwillingness to be committed to any form of value judgement. Thus, when, in the course of a discussion about dispossessed people, the plight of North American Indians was mentioned, it was decided that there was no way of establishing the extent of cruelty imputed to Indians by the white man. This conclusion was based on the following arguments:

1.   Most of the information regarding American Indians is biased, since it was gleaned and selected by the white oppressors.

2.   There is hardly any first-hand evidence by Indians to support their allegations against the whites.

3.   The remains of Indian material culture are merely "archaeological" and not written evidence and, therefore, dubious as a testimony to what really happened. (This last argument is particularly interesting since it is compatible with the idea that thinking could only be accomplished through conceptual representations in verbal or written forms.)

By dismissing non-conceptual ways of knowing, the members set a trap for themselves. Philosophy seemed to them "obscure and not applicable to real life," while non-conceptual facts were regarded as illegitimate sources of knowledge. Between the two areas there remained a very narrow and shaky ground of acceptable knowledge upon which members could safely tread. Irritated by the realization of the restricting conditions they, themselves, set for their discussions, some angry responses were often heard: "Too many people talk too much about matters they know nothing about," or "No point in reading books about things that were supposed to happen or about explanations to things that happened, we must get to know the thing in itself from first-hand experience." How, then, could "the thing in itself" emerge, when almost all its escape routes were blocked by this self-imposed trap?

Emotions were aired and feelings were reported while discussing issues projected in the mass media and particularly on television. It seems that when the subject was, unlike family and friends, remote and impersonal, it induced reactions that were otherwise well guarded. As we explore in the following chapters, personal concerns and strong feelings were usually expressed against the backdrop of mass-media stimuli. Such pretext for unveiling the "essence" beyond concepts was a satirical television show that prompted a general discussion about jokes.

Jokes were regarded as a "survival mechanism" against oppressing regimes, against the establishment, and in times of great social distress or personal anguish. The kind of survivability offered by jocular behaviour was that of the absurd, since that is the "only way to preserve sanity in an impossible reality." Examples from "extermination camps" and "totalitarian regimes" were adduced to demonstrate the comic relief that jokes may offer and to comment about the nexus between jest, depression, and death. John Cleese, the British comedian who was reportedly suffering from acute depression, was mentioned as an embodiment of such connection. While recalling one particular episode of his comedy television series, "Fawlty Towers," where a dead body of a hotel guest is being dragged and hidden and reemerges in various sites, the following remark was made:

— "The fact that John Cleese not only performed in this episode but also directed and wrote it and the fact that he has always been plagued by depression and nervous breakdown—it is therefore significant that he has in fact been questioning, undermining, inducing a feeling of insecurity in himself about the way we live and the society that we live in, that, you said, we would be able to laugh at that quite securely and safely."

Jokes are, indeed, a form of social execution inflicting death on sacred values and taken-for-granted behaviour.[3] This conclusion reached by members led to further observations regarding the shattering effect of jokes on the social order. One such comment was that once a social system is attacked by jokes, "it becomes evident that the sacrosanct and the sacred are no more than social conventions behind which people want to hide because conservation is deeply seated in all of us." Jokes, therefore, are a two-pronged social device, which, while being part of the culture, have the potential to undermine it. Members spoke of jokes as "a threat to our security and a cause for uncertainty" or as "touching upon the unknown." Evidence to support the assumption that jokes tease social order was given in the form of a lengthy discussion about revolution and anarchy.

It was argued that all revolutionaries and anarchists were known to be "extremely serious personalities who lacked a shred of a sense of humour." Once the duality of jokes disappears and the destruction of a social system has reached the point of no return, joking is rendered misplaced and dangerous. "Extremists are scared of jokes because they are uncertain of themselves," said one of the members, and another added "jokes could inflict upon you a sense of nothingness, of not knowing what to expect after the social barriers have been crushed."

This last point is probably the key to the function of jokes within the code developed by the members. Jokes seem to fulfil the role of an intermediary between the highly criticized shield of concepts on the one hand and the luring "essence" to which members strive on the other. Debunking social graces and cultural dictates was one of the main preoccupations of members, but the fear of being exposed to their own basic feelings or lack of them prevented them from facing "the thing itself" without the brokership of jokes, the media, or, as we shall discover later on, certain activities.

Fear of self-analysis was expressed in the attitude towards the professional expertise of psychologists, who were described as "the invaders of privacy and of emotions." This was associated with harsh stricture regarding IQ tests and other areas of opportunities controlled by psychology. It was reiterated that full mastery of one's feelings is a crucial resource that must be defended at all costs. An example of a fictional character whose conduct is a testimony to this principle was found in J. R. Ewing, the protagonist of the television soap opera "Dallas." He was deemed to be in full control of his contradictory feelings and capable of manipulating his environment to preserve his "inner self."

Preservation of self—or, as members called it, "conservation of feelings"—was a cherished idea fostered by members to the extent of saying that dealing with emotions is "a form of risk-taking." That was the reason given to the refusal of members to respond to the suggestion made by one of them to discuss the horrors of the Holocaust. It was maintained that "we probably find it too hard to confront our own feelings, the subject is too close and too personal to us." After a momentary silence the group resumed talking, and a swift switch was made from the highly personal to

the extremes of culture. Myths and legends and the fine distinctions between the two terms were discussed. The sudden retreat into the safe
haven of conceptual hair-splitting was realized by the members, as one of
them put it:

— "If it were 600 years ago, we would have done much the same thing. we
 would have been sitting around here, discussing how many angels could
 dance on the head of a pin, and that's exactly what we are doing at the
 moment."

And another reflected:

— "Well, it is amazing how we have gone whole circle from the birth of a
 baby to the DNA [following a previous discussion to be reported later]
 and now myths and legends."

What enabled these people to take such unguided intellectual tours into
a variety of conceptual landscapes was their ability to apply the code of
the non-importance of context and of its associated cultural devices such
as language to their own experience and life histories. The result was that
in search of the immutable constant, "the essence of things," they managed to abandon conventional parameters of time, space, and meaning and
to reconstruct their own. The following chapters offer a glimpse into this
process of the dismantling and reconstituting of change, social relationships, and relevance.

A possible clue as to the decipherment of the subsequent undoings
could be found in the assertion made by one of the members that: "culture
is an explanation to man's behaviour—but it is only one of many." Since
culture is about learning—values, modes of interpretations, and patterns
of behaviour, and the nature of the activities at the U3A, as we have and
shall ascertain, is about "unlearning "—then the other explanations, beyond culture, ought to be sought in the following. Moreover, if the challenge of "taking it from first principles" is to be met seriously so that
analytic justice can be done with a "folk model," then resorting to the
fundamental categories of time, space, and reasoning seems to serve this
purpose very well.

CHAPTER **5**

Time:
"We All Were Grandchildren"

It is intriguing to note at the outset that the ensuing accounts of life histories were rarely addressed to the model discourse of time so prevalent in ageing research, namely the somewhat arid discussion regarding "continuity" versus "discontinuity" along the life cycle/course.[1] Touching upon many concomitant concepts such as "stages," "disengagement," "integration," and "intergenerational relationships," the debate as to the interconnectedness or otherwise in one's perceived life took many shapes and forms but was almost always underpinned by the basic dichotomy of flow embattled with rapture. Members of the group, while failing to conform to this opposition, offered an entirely novel conception of the whole question of the relations between past, present, and future. They formulated an approach according to which the issue of continuity versus discontinuity is a moot subject, since neither the former nor the latter provides a faithful codification of their world. Rather, it emerged that both concepts were fused into one notion of what might be termed "transversal" or "lateral" continuity (for an explanation of the concept, see Hazan 1985). That is to say that members articulated their knowledge of the world in terms of the persistence and durability of certain key patterns rather than in terms of change. In some way that was a development of the aforementioned abandonment of context and the dismissal of circumstantial environmental influences.

An appropriate introduction to the ways in which this notion was formulated could be dovetailed from the end of the previous chapter—that is, the correlation made between myth and the DNA genetic matter. In both cases, it was argued, the core substance does not change and makes continuity of form and structure possible in spite of transformations in context and content—different phenotypes as well as various cultural manifestations of the same basic myth. The role of myth as a means of transferring experience into an immutable mould was analysed by one of the members as follows:

— "The very fact that humans create myths is a way of trying to explain to themselves something which they noted happened, and trying to relate that something in a way which is going beyond what an animal does."

Myth is thus conceived of as a vehicle for conveying and preserving in its original form a rudimentary experience "happening." Moreover, generating myths is rendered an exclusive human faculty. That observation opened the floor to a discussion of the validity of historical and evolutionary explanations in the understanding of human nature. It was agreed that such models do not offer adequate comprehension of the course of events since "history is contrived and evolution leads nowhere, and, in any case, nothing really changes, it's all appearances."

This last deliberation led the discussion into a cleft-stick position since it suggested a self-contradictory position. On the one hand, it was imbued with a strong tint of fatalism and even predestination, whereas on the other it implied a chaotic, non-deterministic, even existentialistic outlook. This inconsistent appearance could be easily resolved in view of the dual position previously discussed. There was the conviction that the fundamental nature of time is static and unalterable, and alongside it there existed the realization that things, events, and concepts undergo constant change. The two dimensions do not inform each other and, therefore, belong to separate modes of construing experience—basic and surface, reality and phenomenon, truth and appearance.

A possible intrusion of one domain into the other could cause havoc and disarray. Such is the case with induced change and projects that might turn out to be detrimental to their objectives. British party politics was adduced as an example of such a self-subversive process:

— "The point I'd like to make is the one about the paradox you get. I mean, the point about groups having an interest in stability. But what has happened with us—in our economic situation, a tremendous paradox in

British society, whereas the Labour party has become a conservative party, because they want to preserve the structure of society, and the rift, or the thrust of our economic policy over the last 30 years. And, of course, the Conservative party has become a radical party, because they are the ones who want to turn it all over."

The concept of progress as a marker of teleological change was an obvious target for criticism, since it contained the idea of a predetermined career path. The idea of progress was conceived of as the source of almost all vices and was traced back to the fundamental tenets of Christianity, particularly associated with the quest for salvation, namely betterment:

— "Every society is faced with change, and the problem really is to try and make certain changes and cause as little damage or as much good as possible. There used to be a nice nineteenth-century assumption that progress meant everything is getting better and we found to our cost that it doesn't—not always."

— "Yes, but you're now talking solely about Western society, because after all there are vast tracts in the world where change is alien, and they reject it because they try to retain social institutions and education and so on. . . ."

— "Yeah."

— "It seems static."

— "You could argue with the Buddhists that this was one of the reasons why clearly very intelligent societies haven't progressed in the scientific sense in this world, whereas with Christians, they care about being saved, and as soon as you begin saving someone, you're improving."

The praise of Buddhism and of other non-progressive creeds was part of the argument upholding myths as the cornerstones of human existence. As that existence is built on the pervasiveness of universal myths, the historical and geographical boundaries between cultures, countries, and societies are blurred enough to have the evident distinctions between them collapsed or annulled. Unclear also is the springboard in time from which a certain myth gathered its cultural momentum. Both subjects are addressed in the following, which provides yet another testimony to the absence of historical reasoning as well as to the duality of fatalism versus haphazardness. This is the analogy with DNA:

— "When we're thinking of the Genesis story, the Greek story, the northern tribes, and so on, they've all got their idea about how the world started. The strange thing is that what we know now obviously also suggests that there is a period in the development of society where these myths have to be significant sufficiently to persist. You can take them now as you take the DNA—the point at which that mutation in the code becomes stable then persists and is passed on from generation to generation."

"Dallas" was invoked again to demonstrate such a point of mutation, a point beyond which myth, be it ancient or modern, acquires immortal power.

— "Dallas, well—I'm not very well conversant with the latest happenings in that saga, but apparently it has already accomplished some degree of eternity; I mean—it doesn't matter what happens now, it doesn't matter who is going to die physical–biological death, or who is going to be sacked, who is going to resign—this is going to continue and continue forever. It has created its own self-perpetuating form."

However, the temporal realm of the eternal cannot account for everyday life, and a fervent discussion as to the unity or disparity of time worlds spells out again the ambivalent position towards the matter—namely the unison of all temporal perspectives surpassing all kinds of social diversities versus the stark evidence of modern living in multiple universes of time. The conclusion to this quandary is instructive in two respects. First, it draws on the essential metaphoric repertoire of the discussant—the world of biology. Second, it reaffirms the desire to reach to the most fundamental guiding principle of human nature:

— "Well, there's a hole in all this."
— "We all live in one time system."
— "We have lived in a time system about work, a time system of our own immediate families, the time system of the larger family of which that family is a part, and we can think of other sorts of times. They all interdigitate. Nobody lives in one clear time system of his own."
— "Yes, absolutely, there's no question about that. The question is what are the intersections, and does one time system inform another, and if it does—and certainly it does—in what way? When can you possibly complete your family life with your professional life?"
— "No, not your professional life—it goes a long way to running your family life."
— "That's quite true."
— "We talk about you, we, and so on. A thing that I kept wanting to ask is—who are we talking about? Are we talking about the human race as a whole?"
— "We are talking about Western society as we know it. Well, that hasn't lasted very long. I mean, if you had sat there, say, 200 years ago, you

would have been talking about entirely different sorts of times. In other words, these things are to me very reminiscent and very superficial if they're talking just like that—it depends what suits you at a particular time. But there is a problem about time being an issue, you know, something that's worth thinking about. It's obviously a fact. Well, I don't think one can generalize. You have to take a particular society. Think about an urban industrial society, then, what you choose to call a linear or progressive thought has been very strong. But, equally, you could argue that—I don't like the word 'cyclical' because I think by a seasonal and periodical precision—you've got a working day, you've got the shops opening, closing, and so on, all the time there are these structures in there. And, well, it depends where you want to start from; I would have thought the most basic thing is what's innate and ask if there is a definite clockwork. But I don't think that that finishes with children."

The biological solution of circadian mechanisms, while doing away with contextual impositions regulating time, runs the risk of narrowing the gap between man and animal, since they are both governed by the same innate clock-like physiological devices.

The dialectic between nature and nurture, the biological and the cultural, is indeed implicit in the very pursuit of the "thing in itself" and was adumbrated in the unlikely but nevertheless repetitious analogy between myth and genetic matter. Far from merely presenting a complex intellectual dilemma, the issue at stake for the members, as it is for other elderly people, was the choice between a biologically determined identity, which means finitude, and an enduring symbolic presence[2] and culturally constructed self, which can be indefinitely preserved and altered. Time, therefore, had to be renegotiated to have it transformed from a position of absolute control over human life, such as in the case of biological clocks, to being a man-made, manipulable factor. To do this, members had to render the idea of objective time invalid. Bearing in mind the blatant avoidance of any expression of personal feeling, the possibility of resorting to the most obvious alternative to objective time, namely subjective temporal conceptions, had to be circumvented. Members' knowledge of history, archaeology, and current affairs enabled them to construct a personally approved socio-cultural perspective of controllable time.

— "There is a very good reason why we are using train as a metaphor for time. When I say "we," I mean our kind of society—you know, time is running and so on. All this started with the building of railways and then the industrial revolution. The fact that you had to go into the factory at one time—everybody had to go there, because that was the only way in which you could work with people, whereas in a different craft society, when he has finished his meal he gets down to his job, whatever it is, and doesn't look at the clock and say 'Oh, I've got another five minutes before I can start.'"

— "But hasn't the clock become one of the goddesses of time in our society?"

— "It's merely part of our society."

— "Sure."

— "I think it's like many of our mechanical reactions to life. We tend to regard them as gods, such as cars, x-rays, or whatever, when in actual fact they are only really agents. Trains might be slightly different, and I think that what you were saying, that it was in fact the introduction of railway transit, to take an extreme example, which forced the city of Carlisle to abandon its own structure, since, if I remember correctly, it was only 20 minutes ahead of London."

Having established the significance of socially engendered time-structuring devices, members realized that their idea of freedom and independence might be curtailed by adhering to rigid time frames and that the reification of the dictates of clocks might bring them back to the absolute rule of inexorable rhythm.

Controlling rhythm and pace was the subject of many discussions, and the solution of a flexible timetable for work was enlisted to demonstrate it. When in the course of the following exchange a possibility of a recourse to natural body time was introduced, a distinction was made between time and its regulating clockwork. At this point, a shift was made from a circadian, biologically conditioned mechanism to the natural cycle of the elements—sunrise and sunset. This interpretation to objective time seems to be more satisfactory than human physiology, since it is neither terminal nor individual.

— "You do have those people who can work from home or whatever, they seem to have a different timetable. They don't have to be in the office at eight and so on. You've already got—certainly, in my time, we introduced flexi-time. Now, for very interesting reasons, connected with precisely the difficult circumstances of people rushing into the same train to get to the city centre and so on, or occupy the highway, the clock that we're talking about—begins to be less dominating. In other words, what measure of time we use and what signal we use is relevant to our lifestyle and activity as a society."

— "Isn't it easier for us to have a regular clock, an inner clock?"

— "Well, the inner clock is not all that regular, because they did these tests, you know, getting people into a dark chamber for 24 hours."

— "Twenty-five, I think. It's 25 hours."

— "You test some clock and take away the clockwork, it's not very reliable."

— "Well, it depends, but you don't change your clockwork from winter to summer, do you? In that sense I was suggesting that the sunrise and the sunset—the clockwork of ordinary life and foremost human existence, it's sunrise and sunset that determines time."

The natural cycle was no escape, however, from grappling with the personal life cycle. That turf was gingerly trodden upon, as the following brief exchange demonstrates:

— "We all have grandchildren."

— "I haven't."

— "Then we all were grandchildren. We all had grandparents."

This personal aberration was short-lived, and the mention of parents was promptly generalized and transcended to the pragmatic assertions about the contextual underpinnings of time and its cultural varieties:

— "My mother is aged 95. She is pretty amnesic, and I doubt if she could read a clock now. But I can tell the time by her appearance for the next meal."

— "Well, what about in the old days—in the country they didn't have clocks, and it was the animals that told the time for this, that, and the other. Anyway, it keeps on coming back to the thing I said in the first place. All this business of time has to be taken in the context of the particular society and the culture and so on. Because it's there that you get your signposts. And the signposts change from society to society, from culture to culture."

Personal memories were, indeed, widely discussed, not by way of recollections, but through converting the personal to the conceptual. Pondering over the characteristics of memory and reminiscences, members posited their acute awareness of the distinction between the impression of the object and the object itself. It occurred to them that in the age of recollection the two are not necessarily united and possibly belong to different categories of reference, with the memorized object being an immutable fact, while its memory transient and passing. The dialectic between object and memory poses the dilemma of the image of the past in the present in relation to the actual happening:

— "You know, something seems to me particularly significant for us. There was a saying, but it was terribly difficult to know what the saying was—that we change through our recollection."

— "But you can't really remember exactly what it was like. A complete lapse of memory, and there is no way of expressing it."

— "This is also a question of passing through the life cycle. I suddenly met the other day a chap I knew, and we looked upon something differently. One was younger, and we had more energy, and everything is now new."

— "Do you still ever think of somebody as being 'a funny old bastard?'"

— "Yes."

— "Probably under the influence."

— "Yes, sure. But shall you ever remember the occasion of meeting people? If there is anything that will really have a sort of established, objective things—otherwise memory is only very selective. By things I mean a natural artifact that you can record or put into a museum and so on, or something that you measure by some instrument. Whereas the other things that you're saying are something that one feels and thinks—well, if there is anything at all in what that person said, and, therefore, that's the only record you have, and they know that what you say, compared to what you feel, don't quite match up anyway—that time, let alone in recollection, at some later time."

This short discussion was only a preamble to unravelling the secrets of memory. It was evident that members' minds were grossly occupied by those issues to the extent that they even deviated from their customary ban on philosophy and philosophers and found themselves recruiting Heidegger's phenomenological existentialism to fathom their intellectual plight. This plight, as we shall read in the following somewhat long-winded discourse, was grounded in a number of murky areas of knowledge, and it is hardly surprising that it produced conceptual confusion resulting in some uncharacteristically ambiguous and disjointed statements:

— "The essential thing is to have a memory. If you have memory of an event which goes for a while, it is in process, and it's never completed, whatever, then you only have a memory of a memory. So even if it doesn't produce any effect, then you've got it in a different category from the thing that's on-going—it's the business of being and becoming, and there is a switch from the being to becoming, and that is sort of the emerging dominating paradigm and all—not just a question of science but also a very vast philosophical domain. Well—have you ever tried to read Heidegger? I mean, it's the most frustrating intellectual exercise you can engage in. But that was his subject really."

— "Well, yes."

— "Because you judge whether you are going to slow down or speed up."

— "When you think and one very often says of people who live in the country and so on—they are so much more aware of what goes on around them and so on, and obviously these are natural faculties of this, many of which we've just left. Now, coming back to the computer shift—a computer can only record in its memory what is selected to put in. And when you think of the mind as the secret of taking things in, you simultaneously take in things on so many levels that I don't see our selective recording of certain things. The only difference is that, of course, where you earn, your recollection of facts. That's where the computer once it's in there presumably won't deteriorate. But in the sense of the feeling that surrounded that particular experience, what's that part—and there again, of course, the amazing thing is that there are times when you can evoke long-past memories in their vitality—with smells, with fears and hopes. That is why I suggest that it is there—it is recorded in the mind. The question is—how to retrieve it, and how to— you know—develop better faculties."

— "Can you recall it fully, and haven't you interpreted the shape of things you get when some . . ."

— "Yes, I hope you're not recording that."

— "I'm talking about some experience which may go back to very early childhood, where you virtually have a complete—well, print of what you experience there—that there are fears and whatever. Now—that's what I call the natural record. Now, of course, when you recall in a way in which you say—well, you know, thinking about past events you are already putting an interpretation."

— "To judge."

— "How do you know it's complete?"

— "Well . . ."

— "The computer will give you a chance."

— "As a small child it was always a vast chance, the gardens seemed enormous and so was everything else."

— "That's right."

— "But you don't, you see—you don't remember objects, you remember your memories. And this is an entirely different thing. You remember your memories, and in the course of remembering your memories are amenable to all kinds of interpretations and changes."

— "Can you tell me that you see objects? Are you seeing me?"

— "No. Certainly not."

— "Why? Of course. But this induces the whole process that only endorses what I said before: The moment I see you is the moment of forming the memory of you. And—right, I start memorizing you as soon as I see you. And by saying that I memorize you, I mean that I interpret what I see. And this is an unconscious force."

— "I know."

— "Your memories get reinforced on many things by illustration and by other things that you see later. I can remember seeing an aeroplane in 1911. I know when it was."

— "So you can see what . . ."

— "An aeroplane?"

— "In 1911. It made a crash-landing in our village."

— "1911 is a long time back."

— "But I can fix it because we had moved house in the spring, and this was summer. And . . . But my recollection of that aeroplane and its shape and so on—after all, I was only three—is largely conditioned by the shapes of other aeroplanes, I think, that I've seen since."

— "Yes."

— "This is why I don't think that you could really rely upon your own memory."

— "Yes."

— "And don't you often imagine or think that we remember something— but you are not sure, really. Somebody told you about it and said it in such a way."

— "Oh, sure."

— "You're portraying an image. I believe I remember certain things when I was, say, three."

— "I'm not quite sure. I think my mother probably told me, you know."

— "I can certainly remember that one."

— "Yes. But there are certain events which we believe we remember and in fact . . ."

— "I was just going to say, do you think it matters how one argues? You witness something which you thought you saw as in a different time."

— "I meant that other things reinforce the accuracy or inaccuracy of your recollection, of exactly what you saw."

— "I saw exactly that."

— "There was an event—but, whether my recollection of that event is now accurate in any kind of detail, I much doubt."

— "One of the most interesting things I noted is that there are reviews on new history books and there are two levels—the book and the review. This is part of the result of recent research, which means that perhaps events are much less important than we interpreted for a generation which had a completely different point of view. And I'm always fascinated about—you know, someone who saw an aeroplane in 1911. Your view of the state of the world must be totally different from mine, because I remember it from the point of view of being a child, whereas you will remember it from the point of view of being in a much more stable world."

— "You have a childish world-view."

— "That's one way of putting it."

The host of problems raised in this exchange is wide-ranging. What concerns our discussion, however, is the pivotal question that captured the minds of the participants—that is, as the text indicates, the bilateral conversion from experience to memory and vice versa. It was neither experience nor memory that stimulated the debate, but the process of "becoming" in relation to being or, as was gradually revealed, the mechanism of interpretation and its ramifications to the relative importance of memories and facts and to the lack of constancy and durable templates to construct an "event-faithful" narrative. This last point should not be seen in the context of textual presentation which in itself was of little interest to the members, but as markers of their concern with being trusted by others and by themselves. A strong claim for autonomy and self-reliance was voiced in this exchange, and a plea to recognize the general, age-free inability to depend on memory as an accurate mirror of experience was more than implicit. The regression to childhood as the only period where great proximity could be achieved between experience and its recollection was significant in its inherent challenging temptation to dwell on long-past memories. That, however, was not indulged in; instead, a discussion regarding the capacity of people to go back to their roots took place. Again an instant shift was made from the personal to the general, and the issue of being the same person throughout one's life course was elevated to the grand question of "going back to nature" or returning to a previous state of humanness. The conclusion that such a move in time is impossible and that there is no way of remaining the same person was only too predictable. The ending of this debate, however, was rather telling, since it connected the subject of change to social impositions and to personal happiness:

— "The assumption that people can be the same again is a false assumption logically, to begin with. Nobody can be the same again, even in the most stable setting imaginable. And people develop and change, and their way of life is ordered to other times. So the whole idea of returning to nature, of returning to some previous stage, where we used to be different, is preposterous. But I really can't answer that. I mean, the question is, 'Do people want to go back to the previous state?' I really don't know."

— "Are people happy to change, or are they going to be happy to accept present society commitment?"

Elegantly eschewing the component of happiness in that question, members elected to address the factor of social norms and to elaborate on the nagging issue of trust, which was subdivided into personal, mutual commitment and social compliance. The case of the doctor–patient relationship was brought up, as on many other occasions, to demonstrate the difference:

— "It is based not only on trust, but also on compliance with authority. What it represents is a form of trust, of course, But it is not trust in the sense that we mean it, but trust in the sense that—I mean, it is trust in the relation between two people on an equal basis, on an equal level. Compliance with authority doesn't fall under that category at all. I mean, it is like trust in your political leader. I mean—you know that in a way you've got no choice in the matter, and you have to trust your doctor. What else can you do?"

Trust, as already mentioned, was a sore subject, for it implied that the inevitable change—the deterioration in the condition of the ageing members—might have serious repercussions on the trusting attitude of others towards them. The issue as such was never discussed, yet it manifested itself in many behavioural patterns developed among members (see last section of the book) and in indirect references such as the repetitive condemnation of alcohol consumption, which "rules you and drives you to the limits of trusting yourself." "Being under the influence" was held responsible for the most ominous of all losses—that of self-control. Some members even went as far as to state that abstinence ensured their present mental agility. Having extensive medical knowledge, a number of members spelt out the unavoidable psychological and physiological effects of drinking and vividly described its self-destructiveness.

Ascribing deterioration to a self-inflicted external agent of destruction emphasized the predicament of personal choice versus social constraints. This point was pursued under various guises, the most explicit of which was the issue of socialization and the social shaping of a person.

Following a discussion of the educational background of political leaders, members tried to trace the very early effects of social contact on upbringing:

— "At that time your basic socialization is already happening—earlier, you

— really want to go much earlier, and in fact the latest psychological views are, that the thing really goes right back to the baby stage."

— "Pre-baby stage."

— "The socialization factor and which way you get socialized depends entirely on—not entirely, but is dominated by—that early experience. And one thing that I recall on that is—I don't know where I got this from—about the difference between the Balinese culture and many others. The Balinese culture, the people there, the thing that struck the anthropologists was the lack of ambition in the way in which we know it, and the lack of conflict. And that . . ."

— "A great deal of conformity."

— "Yes. And the hypothesis was about the babies already brought up by their mothers in a very different way from what they are with us. In other words, they were as if trying to break the emotional bond as part of a play. And that—well, but there were the details. But the point was that that was meant to be a dominant link between that stage and a later one. We know from delinquent children that again if you've got a bad mother for a baby and so on, that's where many of the problems start."

The highly deterministic view inherent in this discussion was both comforting and disturbing, since it suggested the possibility of resisting change alongside the curtailment of choice and initiative. The following discussion, which contains some rare personal reflections, attests to this dilemma. The joint moulding force of genes and education leaves very little room for personal manoeuvring, but there are enough interstices where decisions can be made and a choice exercised. Such actions of selection can nevertheless be committed only at some critical stages in one's life, and they have long-lasting effects. The role of society is a hampering one, and good intentions unaccompanied by strong will and determination are not sufficient to go against the social order.

— "And I was going to suggest—was your behaviour due to the way you had been brought up in a certain way of trust and responsibility, that you couldn't drink and be unruly?"

— "No, it was just a rational approach of somebody going through Oxford on scholarship money, deciding to succeed. There were two things he could avoid—alcohol and tobacco—and save a lot of money."

— "Yes, but this is really a very important point—that going back to the family, because it can quote only one statistical fact: the number of children of divorced parents tend to divorce themselves much more than children of non-divorced parents. And this is very significant, as far as trust goes, because it proves that there are probably acquired patterns of non-trusting—non-trusting partners, of non-trusting other human beings in the home surroundings. And it is probably true that we can trace trust behaviour throughout the life-cycle back to its origin in the family."

— "When you are talking about youth or earlier—you know, the trustworthiness—the only person that provides trust, I think, is the Lord . . . and what is the principle that—you know—that you expect as necessary that people should become self-reliant and trust themselves, but not so much as others, you know, in our days, because of, you know, national services, social services, all that sort of thing, people get so much. You see, they have special privileges."

— "The younger generation are what they are for two reasons: because they get their genes from us and they got their upbringing from us. So if they're wrong, it's we who are wrong. My experience in connection with help and social services has been that the younger generation is more socially concerned than my own generation."

— "I mean—I wouldn't accept that humanity has been depreciated. I would accept that there are patterns in government which are devalued—and I think we're seeing them at their maximum now."

— "I'd suggest that our values are devalued."

— "Yes. Sure—that's right."

— "But that makes it more difficult for people who are ready, who believe in themselves and then want to develop themselves, because of the pattern of government."

— "We all in some respect are dependent, and so, if it's not easy for us to get expert advice somewhere, consumer legislation must propose something, and that has to protect us."

Instead of advocating abortive attempts to change the world, members fall back on their conviction that interpretation, rather than things as they really are, makes reality. A lesson to that effect is drawn from the study of history in schools. Since there are different "histories," a switch from one to another is not impossible.

— "What about modern historians who emphasize everyday living?"

— "Some of them do, yes, of course. There are exceptions. But this is not the way we used to learn history."

— "True. British historians who teach, I mean, to that end, put an entirely different light on English history. So that dates like 1066 and that sort of thing in our mind—the presentation that is true, it is relatively true to every age."

— "I was a student in public school, and the senior history master was a socialist."

— "In this country the whole representation of history includes successive generations of schoolchildren that study the same material."

— "Yes, that is true, it's possible to make out what teaching makes of people. For example—I mean—my wife is Scottish, and her concept of history is entirely different to mine. Different things or simple facts, like indisputable events, are seen from the other side. An English victory over the Scots is reversed."

But are there really many historical models, or is it just yet another reflection of our change-riddled society? If the multiple faces of history are a mere illusion, then change is not possible, since events in all periods of time answer to the same basic patterning, which is to be found in myth rather than in history. Furthermore, it is not inconceivable to suggest that "history" and even science are in themselves mythical forms of relating to the world. The course, and structure, of the following discussion regarding those issues is self-evident, not only in its bold assertions and conclusions, but also in its construction. That history is reduced to unchangeable myths is an argument already broached, but this particular exchange is composed in a self-corroborative manner to befit this argument. Members discussed history while completely ignoring—albeit being aware of—any chronological, periodical, or regional schema. The content of the discussion, therefore, is in itself a creation of a myth about history, a narrative about—as one of the members put it—"history as a myth":

— "What interests me is the difference between people who are conscious of time and a sense of history and those who are not."

— "Yes. That's very interesting."

— "That to me is a very interesting thing. Is that impressionist?"

— "Is that cultural? In other words, if you can talk about history and come to appreciate this and be interested in that, then that automatically becomes part of your mental equipment, and you take that into account all the time, whereas somebody who has never been taught that . . ."

— "I don't think so. Or is there something else, or something fundamental, or whatever? Because there's no doubt that those people who, whenever they come to face decisions or whatever, in addition to considering the thing as it is, there and then—the situation—would also harp back and forth on what's the effect of time and so on, and others won't do that."

— "Well, I'm wondering whether there isn't something different. But when you think about a civilization where things were changing, but slowly, compared, say, to our civilization during one to two hundred years or more, things were so little different. But then you get to understand that all you could say then was that things are always the same. It was very rare indeed that there was a major change there. Whereas our society is one which has been moving very fast, and, therefore, one is conscious of constant change, and because of that, in turn, this time factor, the historical factor, becomes more important, more prevalent."

— "Is it history or myth?"

— "There's considerable confusion between myth and history. Is not myth often an attempt to explain history?"

— "The origins of history, not so much history itself."

— "Well—yes, if you like."

— "The genesis of history."

— "Yes. Though even in simple societies . . ."

— "It's pre-history really."

— "Or possibly the local priest whose word was handed down by word of mouth from generation to generation."

— "This is a myth, of course."

— "It's a distortion of imperfectly understood history."

— "Of course."

— "So it is."

— "But it's not a deliberate distortion."

— "Oh, no. No. But, then—it's difficult to explain what we don't know regarding the distortion."

— "If you get far enough back, when you haven't got an explanation, then you turn to myth."

— "Yes."

— "Or Godfather in Jesus."

— "That sort of thing is in all cultures, including our own."

— "I think the cross-purposes are between myth and legend, because, I think, a legend is a peculiar kind of history, more precise, but it also has in-built all sorts of misunderstandings."

— "About what happened there."

— "Many distortions."

— "It's a question of degree, rather than kind. The difference is because it's something you enact."

— "Perform."

— "It influences your outlook on life. Of course, we've got our scientific methods, and so on. Those people have some picture of this world around us which isn't strictly what the physicists really are talking about."

— "Which means that here we're talking about two kinds of myths developing—one which goes regardless of man's way of thinking out a problem, and, two, the old ingrained culture that, as you say, all societies have in common—I think it is probably still more evident in Greece than in a lot of places, where the worship of Virgin Mary is very often still closely intertwined with the worship of Athena."

— "Surely all these things go back and come back."

— "The more you read about the history, and goodness knows it's inaccurate enough, any field you get into, the more you will come across some common content."

— "Yes, right."

— "The thing that interests me is, for instance, that casting in bronze emerged in so many different places in the world at about the same time, and nobody has been able to show historical connections between Indo-China and, for instance, the Middle East. When you contrast myth and legend, you're really pulling away two strands of the same piece of work."

— "No, I was merely trying to avoid a confusion between, for instance, in Greece sometimes they would say Zeus and sometimes they would say some king. Well, in that period, some kings are mythical, kings are begotten by gods or demigods, and so on."

— "Yes, but legends . . ."

— "And what is already a myth. But that's merely because you apply our kind of precision of the finer things, which we know well enough."

— "But surely if they were to trace generalities back, they would come to a point where they couldn't go any further, so you stuck in the original ancestor. OK . . . but then, in exactly the same way, you trace back the earliest Pharaohs—when you are short of a word, up pop Greek names."

— "I think it was more in Greece, because you see in this country, if you meet somebody and you say that your name is Chambers, and you say 'are you Chambers?' Well, it was in the same way, if you were a particular small ruler of a small island, then if you had been fathered by Zeus, then you were one-up compared with somebody who had been fathered by a nymph."

— "If you are one up on Zeus, long-anteceded backlog, I mean, we're talking now about B.C. 300-and-something, as compared to B.C.—well, 1200, something like that."

— "Surely there is something rather strange in the fact that history keeps on repeating itself from ancient Egyptians onwards, and the fact that we at the moment are particularly conscious of changes in the technological revolution is to some extent reminding us of the fact that we already have an industrial revolution of centuries ago, which learned how to cope with it, and we have since forgotten."

Disarming history of its chronology brings members yet again to consider time. Only now, with the notion of objective flow of time decidedly abandoned, an alternative definition of time, neither social nor personal, is sought. Whitehead's philosophy and latest technological advances affecting work and life are combined to provide a conceptual and empirical frame within which the basic unit of time could be identified as "event." That event, so it transpires, is also the nearest term to the elusive "the thing in itself":

— "But you realize that objective time is a very recent thing, because that really goes back to the fourteenth or fifteenth century—the navigation and so, when time and map in the objective sense emerged."

— "There's the opposite. If law is taking over right through the process, and, if you like, in philosophical terms, the Whitehead concept of processes is the primary thing that is now dominating all the sciences. And the business of objective time as a digital clock and so on, typically for the physicist this is a question of events. It's not time, it's nothing in itself an abstract—this is again the events only in the case of events of extremely short duration. This business of time as an abstract thing is actually of very short duration. I think that, if anything, it is likely to give more, I mean that event thing, into general culture, because we will get much more flexibility rather than being dominated by time like in the industrial period where you got everything, clockwork and chains and working from nine to five and so on. As you get more and more doing things in one way or the other, not going somewhere but being in contact over television or whatever, all these things again slip back and your life becomes dominated by events, as it should be. We have technology which is very broadly distributed. But the technology is now in the hands of people with completely different conceptual frameworks. Whereas in 1911, shall we say, the technology was basically in European hands, with a certain world-view. The men behind the gowns are now people with completely different world-views, in the sense that, clearly, your point of view of living is very different if you are a follower of Homeini, if you are an American or Chinese. And yet, the technology and the capacity that everyone wants to give each other is universal. But the wealth of the frameworks change beyond recognition, from Protestants reading the Anglo-Saxon chronicles, and what would you say about technology, it really comes into that. Because their attitude towards death is totally different. When life was a matter of 25 years, if you were lucky, then it was on such an event that it ended, and the really very matter-of-fact way in which reference is made to the death of prominent figures in the Anglo-Saxon chronicles who have none of the tearing of hair and weeping and so on that you will get now. This is quite in contrast with the present situation."

But are those discrete events fundamentally different from one another, or is there a pattern of structural, lateral continuity uniting them? That question had been addressed previously, and a suggestion of human universals underlying events was made. The following exchange adds another dimension to this discourse. This is the facet of age and particularly of old age. If human behaviour is guided by the same code, then no significant differences could be found either between generations or between the same age group in different historical periods. It would seem a contradiction in terms to observe vast diversity in apparent experiences and maintain that real change does not take place. A resolution of this seeming paradox proves to be of a special importance to elderly people, since it might impinge upon their ambivalent attempt to forestall change while realizing its thrust.

— "If there aren't universals, we would be unable to suggest principles of behaviour. I can tell that, for example, my mother and my children—I can see many great similarities, suggesting a universal experience. But there is a very clear difference, because in my mother's case her behaviour in childhood and in old age spells the same patterns as my children's, yet circumstantial modifications throughout a lifetime suggest completely different experiences."

— "You mean that fundamentally human nature is composed of universal components which you can find in most societies and all cultures, but individual or vernacular life circumstances make human beings behave in different ways, and eventually . . ."

— "That's what they say."

— "Yes. And at the end of the day you can't really see the roots or the rudiments of what has evolved afterwards. I would second that point of view, certainly."

— "There are many of us in the ageing age-group, but I think it made none of us people in need until the Second World War, there were many more problems . . ."

— "I don't think that problems are the basis for the continuity of experience. I think that maybe with the advent of computers and systems of recording and recall and selective recall, future generations may be much better able to document what happens in the ageing process. But the problem is whether in fact the large number of 75-year-olds are really effectively as old as 75 was 20 years ago. This is the crucial question. Most people talking about the impact of an older society talk as if the competence and ability to contribute of a 75-year-old has been the same in all times."

— "That clearly is the case."

— "There's a campaign coming from Stanford. They produced a book on ageing, about 4–5 years ago, in which they brought together a lot of evidence—no doubt, very selectively chosen—suggesting that, as it were, the 75-year-old today may be much more like the 70-year-old of 30 years ago. And if that's so, both physically and mentally, then the people who are running around, tearing out their hair because of the explosion of the ageing population, are really fussing far too much."

— "I think this outcry about a world overpopulated by elderly people is a form of social bigotry, because what has really happened, the message is not that we are going to have more elderly people, the message is that we are going to be over-populated. And it's very very easy to cast the blame on the elderly, of course, notwithstanding the evidence that we have now that elderly people, even in very advanced age, can function just as well as younger people, even better."

Reassuring themselves that their old age is a better one than that of previous generations and that overpopulation is the real problem and not the increasing mentally and physically fit ageing sector, members had to address a pressing question: Why retire? The answer provided contained a member's cursory life review and eliminated all the obvious factors for retirement but one. It negated the idea of obsolescence, the attribution of incompetence, and the insinuation of senility. Conversely, members prided themselves on their acquired wisdom, voluminous experience, and successful leadership. This last quality of leadership is, indeed, the force that determines the turning-point of retirement. As the following suggests, old age was not considered to be a phase of thwarted abilities or inadequacy. Quite the contrary—rather than making concessions to old age, it was deemed a time of brave and just decisions to assume an overall social responsibility to the young.

— "You do learn tricks, and you have to know how to do them. You know, when it takes quite a lot of time, and you ask quite unscrupulously about the ideas of younger people. And this is how you get clever. Looking back on my own life, I realize perfectly well that the new ideas I have were drying up by the time I was 40 or 45; as I get older they dry up even faster."

— "Mind you, they were still enough, say in the next ten or dozen years after that, to make me look to taking leadership, and after that I was joking, because I have learned the tricks and borrowed ideas from my juniors, and without any suspicion of being unscrupulous, go on being thought to be in the leadership. I mean, I had to say to myself quite firmly: Look, 65 is the time when you go. And maybe you could still be a better man than the man who would succeed you, but you can't go on doing that sort of thing, and you could be better if you led him in truth. And, I mean, I think we all make conscious decisions of that kind, but we do also realize that it is so hard to follow them."

— "We don't realize, in fact, that if we carry on after 65, that we wouldn't be quite as good as that younger person."

— "Yes. Yes."

— "And that wouldn't do."

— "The younger person gets frustrated."

— "Yes. That's a good point. I mean, the younger person ought to be let through, and if older people are going to go on, then they ought to be accepting the idea that the younger people ought to move to the front of the stage."

— "They expect the older people to adopt ideas, and I think it's the same thing, the older people must expect that their own success could generate the ideas which they try to apply. Otherwise, you are going—you are just going to admit that the revolution of today is the reaction of tomorrow, and unless you overcome that attitude by applying the ideas of those who create them, this will be true."

— "Yes. You know how many times one heard somebody, a very distinguished person, going on about chairing this and that organization, and taking the lead on various committees. Being so wonderful. But that always is going to be like that because you ought to be saying: Do I mean that he is wonderful? Or do I mean that he at 80 is astonishing, is he still so alert a man like me? And I do think it behoves people in our age-group, and one ten years younger than mine, to understand that, however competent you may be and whatever mistakes you juniors may make, that we have to go."

— "That is perfectly true. This is the point. My philosophy has always been, if somebody asks me a question—should I help him or let him find the answer himself."

— "Yes."

— "Whereas there are a lot of people who are going to say: take the easy way out, and just give him the answer without thinking."

— "This is a way of teaching a person to assume responsibility. Because if you give him the answer, then you are responsible for the consequences."

— "Quite."

— "Of whatever course of action he takes."

— "Yeah. Right."

Seeing themselves as the *avant-garde* of society, setting an instructive example of leadership to the rest, members renounced anything associating them with their past, such as professional status, school reunions, and idle reminiscing. This is probably the reason why after all their juggling with time—stretching, shrinking, and transfixing it—they engaged in the ultimate debate on that subject—a discourse on the discourse about time. The emergent conclusion, as can be seen in the following, is that except for some practical purposes, time is an empty concept not worth wasting time on.

— "Anyway, tell us, when we talked about circadian rhythms, and again one has to be aware of the fact that there is a vast number of chemical and other drugs going on there and they are all ticking at slightly differ- ent times, and when we use that term, it's never a simplification. But then you got another thing, I mean, some people say they feel brightest at mid-day. And I know that the early hours of the morning one feels lowest, and so on, so we all have these various biological things, and they continue all the time. How far you can dissociate yourself from them depends on what we are talking about. I mean, in terms of abstract thinking, in terms of infinity, there's obviously many infinite times. So, I'm not sure really what we want to focus on in talking about time."

— "This is the main problem with time, you see, being so elusive and so abstract, you can very rarely transform it into the pragmatic level."

— "And why should I?"

— "I mean only if it's for some purpose. But this is trivial, it is really irrelevant."

— "Yeah. Well, I would agree. Yes. They are definitional well, futilities, in a way."

— "That's a good word. We're just indulging in a standard senior commu- nal post-graduate conversation."

— "It's entirely unconnected with uses as well as realities."

CHAPTER 6

Space:
"We Are All White Middle-Class—
What the Hell
Have We Done About It?"

Whereas the notion of the event is to be seen as the indivisible chronological unit, the "atom" of time, it is the concept of equality that will be regarded as the "molecular," too-often decomposed essence of social space. Obscurity shrouds them both—the former being covered with layers of concepts and theory, the latter buried under the social edifices of class divisions, inequity, and political conflict. As they did in the case of time, so members devoted numerous discussions to the unveiling of their conception of social space. There is an interesting inconsistency between the material to follow and the orthodox view of the importance of territoriality and known location in the life of the elderly. The abundant literature on the effects of environmental conditions (see, e.g., Lieberman & Tobin 1983; Gubrium 1973) such as housing, community facilities, and residential care is a testimony to the belief that the old are attached to place in the same way as they are assumed to dwell on the past. In spite of ethnographic evidence suggesting the diminishing significance of territory in the construction of meaning in later life,[1] the concern with the threat of "relocation" on the adjustment of the elderly is overwhelming life (see, e.g., Lieberman 1974; Tobin & Liberman 1976). Notwithstanding the social reasons for the prevalence of that perspective, it should be noted that it indicates a high measure of context-bound interpretations of ageing, despite some strong evidence to the contrary. The following should serve as yet another support to the argument that the construction of social space among aged people could be a far cry from being conditioned by an immediate context of inhabiting certain territorial and social loci. In fact, what is presented suggests the opposite, namely the demolition of social barriers and the collapse of cultural boundaries. This is an avenue already explored in chapter 5, and it follows the same quest, to delve into the heart of the matter and to unearth the "thing in itself." The rearranging of social space is to add another dimension to this pursuit.

In a group that boasted a knighted member, it was intriguing to hear a strong denunciation of formal forms of address and titles. Indeed, among themselves, members communicated on first-name terms. Not denying the importance of gestures and etiquette in smoothing out cultural communication, they objected to the ascription of any objective merit to social distinctions. This was due to the observation that "society is not an entity" and that social structure is a reflection of the class system that is "artificial and should not exist." Since the class system is stagnant by nature and society undergoes constant change as the divisions between the classes are meant to be the core of that society, the conclusion must be that the whole social system is defunct and inconceivable. This practical reasoning was further developed to suggest that visible—or, rather, audible—class distinctions are a matter of linguistic differences that can be imitated, adopted, and, in any case, acquired. Such distinctions in forms of talk, accent, twang, and dialect are insufficiently important to mark substantive differences among people. This argument was taken to its extreme through a series of comments regarding the British political system of the day. The then prime minister, Margaret Thatcher, was harshly criticized for her pretence to emulate the upper classes and for her class-system-sustaining policies. The demise of Arthur Scargill, the then militant miners' leader, however, was a cause for joy and gloating. He was blamed for abusing the class system by generating false images of his own working-class people as belligerent, irrational, and extremely restricted in their aspirations. As one of the members put it, "How misleading it is to think that all working-class people are interested in is pubs." As ultimate evidence for the argument that class distinctions are not real, the case of adopted children whose behaviour mirrors that of their social parents, rather than that of their biological ones, was brought up.

Here, in a very similar manner to the deliberations concerning time, the struggle between life-long convictions, and the language expressing them on the one hand, and the nascent urge to do away with such convictions on the other, was only too apparent to members. The solution, as with previous discussions, was sought on the safe ground of recommended action and the pursuit of pragmatic thinking rather than on the turbulent waters of intellectual discourse. Once the idea of equality was agreed upon and was accorded the status of a "first principle," suggestions were made as to its possible implementation. Such was the teaching experience related by one of the members:

— "I had experience of teaching in a comprehensive school where there was a 50-percent immigrant population of Black and Indian and so on. And the West Indian students were, on the whole, non-achievers. Later I was teaching further education; I was teaching child development amongst other things. I was asked by all the teachers 'Please, please, please will you ask, will you stress to the West Indian students, that they must, as mothers, talk to their children?' You see, they do not talk to the under-fives. And this is where the trouble starts. In other words, the culture, and the people, and so on."

Appropriating equal opportunities was hailed as the cure for most so- cial maladies, but the realization that problems of equality in education were embedded in culture rather than in the distribution of resources ren- dered the practical approach untenable. Other discussions on education and the provision of equal opportunities only served to bolster this view and to furnish it with further evidence. At this point it must be observed that the kind of equality that members had in mind was not of a relativistic nature. It simply advocated the belief and the wish that all human beings can strive for the same set of standards determined and maintained by contemporary Western values. In that respect, rationality, science, and modernity overrode the dismissal of those themes in other discussions with idealistic overtones. The world of pragmatism, unlike the universe of ideas, is thus rigidly ordered and rigorously regulated according to the principles of social evolutionism and enlightenment. At the top of the pyramid is the benevolent colonial white who offers the natives a helping hand to climb up and join him. The striking gulf between the routine, pragmatical pattern of practice and critical reflexivity ("first principles") became particularly evident when professional experiences were dis- cussed. As already mentioned, those were very rare occasions. However, when they emerged, the split between the social commitment to one's occupational identity and the adherence to views and values that no longer inform that identity became unavoidable. As one of the members stated: "You can't always go back to first principles." This split, which finds further expression in the self-contradicting combination of subscribing to a form of Western cultural ethnocentrism (this chapter) while at the same time rejecting the doctrine of progress (chapter 5), indeed cuts throughout this chapter. The following is an example of this split. It presents the socio-cultural odds that shaped members' lives against the dissolution of conventional perspectives:

— "The opportunity, even at home, to read, and read extensively as much as you can, depends on having something to read. No matter what's in the school library. It absolutely astonishes me that some of the first generation of recently freed African dependencies, of Britain, anyway, are people who have managed to surmount the enormous disadvantage they must have had."

— "Yes."

— "Of doing their academic background. Only schoolteachers think that the majority of learning is done in school. It isn't. It's done outside. And the opportunities for these chaps were far less. The first Minister of Health in independent Nigeria was and is a friend of mine, a Nigerian. And that— you may be astonished at the extent of his knowledge in his medical speciality and the degree of his insight, and yet he still had some of the prejudices that it becomes extremely difficult to get round, because, I think I said the last time, that you cannot reason back, eh, forward from first principles on every issue that comes before you. You only have the time and the energy to do that in a few examples, and most of the rest of your answers come to be conditioned by the prejudices within which you've been brought up."

— "I agree. Sorry, what you meant brought out in a way my experience as a consultant in a hospital which had for the most part Indian immigrants as junior staff. Leaving out the fact that they in India had practised medicine in a different way, which we didn't realize—we sometimes blamed them for doing their best. Nonetheless, it was very clear that such people were not going to have the opportunities in Britain to obtain the education they ought to be taking back home to India with them. With that in mind, as an example I always used to try to direct them to the next job—to somewhere where they can't take it away. They would meet Cambridge consultants, impress them with their ability, walk into a teaching hospital, and get the same opportunities as home-grown graduates would. It was quite impossible to get them into Cambridge direct, or to any other teaching hospital direct. But the background in India of the medical profession seemed that if one had to go out and try and negotiate and arrange a post-graduate education and exchanges with the post-graduate school of Hammersmith with one or other of the Indian post-graduate institutes. Incidentally, that was close to the new capital of the Punjab, Chandigar, which was some sort of artificial city that has developed to a population of 150,000 in a matter of a few years and has a beautiful new hospital. And that system of rationing, the care they were able to give to the public in need, was to open the doors of the casualty department first thing in the morning and close it late at night. And they told me all about this, and it seemed to be extraordinary what they were doing for the population of a city of that size. That bears out what you were saying."

— "Yes."

— "The attitudes are different."

— "Yes."

— "And the attitudes arise simply from the conditions in which they have been brought to this point."

— "And the British are substantially responsible for it."

— "Well, the question of attitudes. There was an interesting article in *The Guardian* a couple of days ago, I think, from the teachers or some union. Somebody from there wrote about the unexpected sort of finding when they tried to make their case in the newspapers by advertising. The result was quite stunning, because they had a vast number of abusive letters from the public. And they said that the real thing there is that the image of the teaching profession among the ordinary public is very low indeed. Now, the thing that strikes me about it is that factors of this kind really influence the way in which the education is affected and so on. And one thing which wasn't made clear from this article was whether most of the abuses came from England and not from Scotland and Wales, as I would have expected."

— "But, it is this, you see—I mean, if you have that attitude, then you don't have achievers. And that's when you get the trouble in the large comprehensives and so on. And coming back to the West Indians, you see, by contrast, you can be in a disadvantaged situation. I'm thinking now of the Indian immigrants—where, because learning has been very important, so all those children perform well, because their parents give them the chance, encouragement—in fact, make them."

— "Yes."

— "Whereas lots of indigenous problems because of learning and so on are considered to be of no consequence at all."

— "Where appropriate, which is the thing I used to encounter in the North, when you say someone is a sort of all right for the working class."

— "That's right."

Achievement, competition, and success were acceptable yardsticks for one's accomplishments, provided they reflected a starting-off situation of equal opportunities and non-discrimination. Excessive competitiveness as induced by certain educational methods was criticized for its perpetuating effect on the social system:

— "I think one of the worst examples I've seen of that—the difficulties, the social difficulties that competitiveness can produce—is in Mauritius, where they have at age 11 an examination of schoolchildren which is going to determine that small fraction who were to go on to further education; for the rest there was nothing but cutting sugar-cane. And the feeling of competitiveness was simply dreadful."

— "But the eleven-plus only differed from it to a degree, didn't it?"

— "Well, yes."

The fact, however, that some Afro-Asian immigrants to Britain made it to the top called for a non-evolutionary explanation. This was offered by proposing a compound success formula consisting of "energy" and social connections. It was implied that the standing of the group members could be accounted for in the same vein.

— "I was thinking about what you were saying about the success of immigrants. Couldn't it be just a question of energy?"

— "Assuming one wants to improve our society. One wants in some way to change it, usually. You need a certain amount of leverage to do so. The other thing, of course, the very fact that we are here in this room, I'm afraid, implies that we are all white middle-class and have got the time and money to be here."

— "But maybe it's just energy levels, that some people have got more energy than others, and therefore some throw that energy about."

— "Well, it's obviously a factor. I mean, why is somebody a prime minister rather than somebody else? But, if this were so, and it was a question of energy, it implies that you ought to take a simplistic view of our society, which is not very open. Whether it's the old school tie, connections, or the ability of manipulating the environment in which you are—when you move from one country to another, all that is usually causing the big delay."

Having quashed, and not for the first time, the evolutionary stance, it behoved members to reinvestigate the origin of man and to reestablish the commonalities rather than the differences between people. DNA is again a panacea for many scientific mysteries, but conclusive answers to major questions cannot be found. However, the very display of scientific knowledge is sufficient to ensure the possibility of a future solution. In any case, DNA reemerges as one of the versions of the "thing in itself."

— "I think it's more likely that there are a number of places of creation and we've got several origins. What that means later on is too difficult, perhaps obviously, to put into words."

— "But there is evidence of *Homo sapiens* evolving from one place to several lines."

— "I am suggesting to you that there was a continuous process of *Homo*, whatever it is, and at a particular point the *Homo sapiens* comes off."

— "Doesn't this happen at a particular point? I mean, there has been discussion in the past as to what exactly constitutes a species of the genes of *Homo*, as distinct from that of apes. As I understand it, this gene reacts in the development—a very slow, obvious development of the chin."

— "Well . . ."

— "This has been the most important physical development that happened at one time, or at a point in space."

— "But there was at some time a change in DNA. Because that's what we inherited. Now, it's possible that the same change could have occurred in a lot of different places and countries. It's also possible that it could have occurred in one place, and subsequent modifications, which have occurred in a lot of separate places. I mean, some of us have black skin and some of them have yellow skin."

— "It's all possible that the species developed in many places at similar or different times, but only one particular example survived."

— "Oh, yes, but then that still takes you back to the one point."

— "Only one . . . one."

— "I don't know if you lightly dismiss this as being improbable, but I say, 'why?' You've got nearly a million years, more or less incredible hypotheses, and probable hypotheses, and I would say that on the whole a probable one."

— "But you're saying there's evidence."

— "I said hypothesis."

— "Well, since you . . ."

— "Since we have identical DNA in numerous combinations, you have got to have a number of different places in which their identical combination could emerge, and there are millions of possible combinations."

— "Now, there again you are over-simplifying things. You don't have to have identical DNA. We know that all the time the DNAs vary in small sequences and so on. All the time one set or a another of modifications keeps on coming up now in the current work."

— "*Homo sapiens* is where you actually begin to use the brain in a somewhat different and more sophisticated way than before. And, therefore, it's not just DNA, but what use you make of your environment."

— "DNA is going to determine what you get in the way of brain."

— "That is true."

— "That's right."

— "But DNA, then, what do you say it's for? We don't know that either."

— "Quite. I mean, how are they identical to what we have now? In what way do they vary, to what extent are other variations possible?"

— "They become active with the years."

— "Of course. And there is a point at which DNA variants were diverging."

— "It's amazing how we started."

Being inconclusive on the subject of the synchronized mutation moment of the various DNA pools around the globe, members turned to its twin model for explaining the origin of things—myth. Swift comparative journeys across ancient Egypt, Christianity, and contemporary living were made in order to relate human behaviour to one generating force:

— "You know, the ancient Egyptians, for a couple of times a year at least, had a sort of tradition which was the proper way to behave. And most of that time, as in the Christian Church, I suppose, people purporting to be behaving according to the standards that worked. It was still there, and it only got slowly modified. Something like 3000 years. It had pretty well gone by the last Pharaoh, but it's very interesting, this sort of change goes on and on. Nobody knows when it started, and I think one of the most interesting things about reading the history of different cultures is to find how much of a common sort of mess there is from which you start. Some people start one way, and some people start another. I think that is common because if you want to take it at length to start talking about creation myths, much of this out of necessity must relate to cosmic events. And a number of these events are recorded at similar times throughout the world. The one that springs to mind was, was it not Nathan who fought a battle during which the sun stayed in the same position for ten hours and then set in the same direction from which it had risen? The same thing was reported in South America, except, of course, it was night there."

— "Do you think that's just a coincidence?"

— "Yes, I do."

— "Rubbish. Forgive my crude expression."

— "Well, crudely, what I'm suggesting is that the earth probably had a near-miss with a meteor or something and was thrown off orbit. But, you know, there's a certain amount of evidence in favour of that happening at that time. I give this as an example."

— "Yes. there's a lovely quotation in Breary's latest book, from a press report of that cricket match when everything was turned upside down, and it was a letter to the press, which said the reporter said that, no, he'd seen the television, and he'd seen Breary carefully placing the ball, and then looking up at the sun, and apparently instructing it to move."

[*Laughter*]

Since myth and DNA were established as the origins for universal human behaviour, they were held responsible for many perplexing questions. Thus violence was attributed to genetic disorders, and so were language acquisition, gender differences, and musical propensities. The unavoidable logical conclusion of the priority given to heredity over environment was that there are no fundamental differences between social groups and cultural units. Thus any distinction between "us" and "them" is unjustified. In a discussion about football violence (see chapter 7) one of the members pronounced passionately that "we are them, there is no real difference between us." So much so that poor environmental conditions cannot suppress high sensitivities and sublime preoccupations such as reading poetry:

— "Did anybody see the poetry programme on BBC 2 the night before last?"

— "In a very bad background as you would describe, in the way of living conditions, education, and everything else, and in the most fantastic poetry of every kind, and the people are going in their hundreds to listen to it and take part in it. I was amazed. It was a marvellous programme."

The spurious nature of social difference is stressed by the fact that the mass media transcend cultural and political borders and create a "global village":

— "The television, that impressive thing—I mean, the way that it dictated ideas and could manipulate things, or the powers behind the CBS, which I see now. But, you know, it's going on in this country, even though we pretend that we are different from the Americans—you only have to think of the behaviour of some of the people in the media. Just happened this week, after we've seen television of those poor girls who were taken from their parents—shocking people. The look on the faces of those girls, only hours away from that sort of ordeal."

— "You could see they were on the verge of another breakdown. We could see it on their faces."

— "Yes."

Another testimony that was especially germane to members' life experience was the educational system of public schools and, in particular, boarding institutions. This breeding-ground of the British upper classes was conceived to be a coercive mechanism that was capable of processing any human input into the desired output. Here personal memories heavily impinge on the formulation of present attitude, and the following description of a member's boarding-school days helps to demonstrate how a small crack in the system (namely the mixing of day-students with boarders) widened and developed into the decisive current stand regarding the collapse of all social barriers. This could be partly explained by the members' realization that the whole institution was a feigned social vehicle based on pretence and coercion:

— "The anti's, of course, regard the whole thing not as a hot-house society, but as a sausage machine—to some extent they may have a point there. What does interest me—and, in fact, what has been customary to some extent—is a combination of a boarding-school and a non-boarding-school where you have two different societies intermixing. One—the boarding-school society, which presumably in the case of a pure boarding-school is so arranged as to keep idle hands from mischief apart from anything else, and the boarding-school which takes day-boys, who go home at four o'clock and take no part in the social activity whatever, usually because of difficulties in transport etc., as much as anything else. And who appear to have no roots at all. I mean, they are actually at home, they've got their families, society, and so forth. But the two systems do not appear to have been defied at all in the personal experience that I've heard."

— "Aren't we perhaps underestimating the resilience—I think—of young people, who are not quite sponges, as we imagine them sometimes. They do in fact select, and they do sieve their experiences, as far as the mix of day-boys with boarders is concerned. Incidentally, I think that the bounds between the two elements considerably affect the outcome. I think, if you have a day boarding-school with a small day element, or the other way round, I think the view could be taken that in fact the two things—what's the word?—you know, cross-fertilize each other and enrich each other's experience rather than stupefy or impoverish it."

— "I think that was probably the original object of the scheme, but as with the experience of comprehensive school, this can work or go disastrously wrong."

— "Isn't where it's gone disastrously wrong a question of confusion of roles as well? Because, years ago, certainly when I was very small, role-playing was much better defined—say you had a role as a schoolboy, and you knew from the stories you read how that schoolboy behaved. And to some extent life was very possible, because people all acted as parodies themselves; I mean, it was only when I grew older in school that I realized that some of my masters, to make life simpler, pretended to be schoolmasters."

— "You realized gradually, as you grew older, they were much more intelligent than you thought they were when you first arrived."

— "That's right."

— "I think I only discovered that when I came up to Cambridge, and the term headmaster came. On the other hand, I have noticed that with our own children, this concept of headmaster already coming up at O-level plus, and then we shouldn't possibly count him in different roles."

— "You know, I don't think your mixed public-school experience is necessarily standard, because I went to Bedford, which was a school where about one-third were boarders and two-thirds were day-boys. And they did mix. Not as much as might have been useful, but they did mix. Then, of course, that was because the day-boys were predominantly within cycling reach."

— "I can only hope to—really, I think—I admit, one swallow doesn't make a summer, and the mix in the schools that I'm thinking of in particular is precisely the opposite of the one that you quote. Transport problems are considerably different, because it's just about within motorcycling reach, which means that only the over 16's can stay on."

— "We had a different experience, because our boys went to the boarding-school from the local school. One became a day-schooler after O-levels and did A-levels, and the other two became day-schoolers at 13 when their voices broke, so that situation penetrated the state system. And they all complained for the first term. They didn't know their own classmates as a group. But they very quickly got over that, no problem at all. They adapted extremely well."

Lack of present social consensus brings about an increasing range of educational choices; however, the function of any such system has not altered.

— "If this is unacceptable, it is a relatively new thing, isn't it coming back to the sausage machine? You could say the school, the educational system, was a sausage machine, and everybody 50 years ago broadly agreed on what a sausage was."

— "There was at least some sort of consensus. But there is much less consensus now, and, therefore, there must be tremendous confusion in sausage machines."

— "Yes."

The genetic challenge to the idea of equality was met on numerous occasions. Retaining their belief in the role of heredity in engendering human diversity, members still upheld the conviction of equal opportunities and the insignificance of racial differences. Universal justice was the link between genetic hierarchy and the idea of equality. The lines of the following attest to the irreconcilable contradiction between evolutionary persuasions suggesting progress and the tenacious insistence on equal rights and common immutable justice:

— "People believe so much in rights. I think your philosophy is to say that everybody has to have equal opportunities, and everyone should be equal before the law, and there should be equal justice. But somehow if you ventured to suggest that there may be genetic differences between people, someone immediately assumes that you are of the view they're not entitled to justice or opportunity or anything else."

— "One of the interesting things, I think, is that whereas the Chinese, the Indians, the Europeans, all have definite mathematical and ethical culture, and they've taken different forms but the intellectual attainment is there. It does seem to be a certain amount of evidence of a narrower bank of intelligence and ability, certainly in Africa south of the Sahara, where, as far as I know, in terms of architecture and so on, they've found very little. I don't think they had the wheel before other people got there, before either the Arabs or we got there. Another thing is, that doesn't mean they're not entitled to justice or anything else."

— "No."

The self-evident conclusion of cultural ethnocentrism did not, however, escape the attention of members. As one of them put it, "We ought not to be too condescending about past cultures, since we live in a world of different values and yet people are starving." This was a statement made in the wake of a discussion condemning the alleged cruelty of the North American Indians. Such attempts to offer rational explanations condoning or understanding other people's unacceptable behaviour to Western society were numerous. It would seem that members were only too pleased to find environmental or culturally conditioned explanations that might circumvent the need to rely on genetic or evolutionary interpretations of human nature. The nature of human nature captured the interest of members to the extent that almost any discussion contained some overt references to the question of the essence of mankind. Usually a point of social criticism would be made, to be followed by an explanation in the vein of the notion of basic equality and cultural relativity and to be concluded with an observation suggesting some general trait of humanness. Such discourses could be interpreted as dialectical attempts to reconcile the two types of identity projected by members—that of a practically minded, socially involved "white middle class" and that of idealistically oriented people upholding humanistic values. The course of the following discussion provides a good example for this process. Beginning with a severe condemnation of "social parasites" such as "hippies" and idle youth, it proceeds to remove the criticism on relativistic grounds, only to find itself engaged in meeting another challenge to the idea of equality—that of war. A way to settle the differences between the diversiveness of symbolic forms of collective identity and universal egalitarianism is finally sought in the will of all humans to survive, even against the odds of inexorable conditions of existence. The conclusion sparks off a new flame of anti-establishment indignation, and so on and so forth:

— "I think that people believe that what you say is the way that you say it, and what you do is the way that you do it. Could I suggest that possibly this concept is false?"

— "You have these hippies, who have been trying to learn that being swept out, they go to somewhere else, time and again. How do you explain their grouping? They have withdrawn from society, as I've seen it, and yet they want free handouts from society, because I think that's the only way they live. I find that very interesting, that they want their way of life, but want all that this country can give them."

— "Well, yes."

— "I wouldn't for one moment justify their behaviour. I certainly don't sympathize with them. Nevertheless, they are not the only sector in our society who makes similar demands. I mean—if we are talking about the class system in this country, or in any other country for that matter, based on God-given privileges, people claim all kinds of benefits from society, and they get them as long as they are legitimized by social institutions. Therefore, they are outcasts and outlaws. But, were they legitimized by social institutions, I suppose they would have been on a par with other sectors in our society."

— "It is like the question of women who demand equal rights with men and give up women's privileges, or not be equal."

— "Yes, sexual discrimination is really shocking in this country."

— "Isn't it a confusion between equality and identity? The same goes with ethnic relations."

— "Well, I don't know."

— "Most men trade upon the outcome of what has always been regarded as manly."

— "True. True, of course it's true."

— "What shocked me—when was it? . . . two weeks ago, I think—the victory won by that Irish boxer—I don't know his name."

— "And the way that the whole people, the nation, rounded around him as a symbol of their identity."

— "I mean, let's face it—the object here is peace in Ireland—if he can achieve what nobody else can."

— "Oh, yes."

— "For people need success, and this is the curious thing about success— just as everybody says it: the success of little units. Football teams are very important for the people of Liverpool, because there is a lot of unemployment there and this is the thing that they would hold on to, which is a huge success and being better than anybody else."

— "But it's much more than success. It's victory. It's not only success, because you can talk about scientific success as an intellectual achievement, and they are not as praised as the accomplishment of that boxer. It is victory. It is war. It is really war. And he has won a war. And that's how people view it."

— "But what about the hundreds of millions of people in the world today who are starving and dying, many of them in refugee camps in Crimea and other places like that; there is no victory like theirs. There is not even enough to sustain a physical life there."

— "Absolutely."

— "Which makes intellectual activity impossible. When you are really sort of picking the grains of wheat such as the E.E.C. and not thinking about where they go—they go in their own mind, not somebody else's. The governments in Europe are organizing a reduction of agricultural articles, with hundreds of millions of people starving."

The state of the starving world ignited some fervent discussions on the social distribution of economic resources and on the personal commitment of members entailed by it. Attitudes towards food consumption in the form of dietary habits seemed to reflect the moral dilemma of the injustice of affluence in the midst of great deprivation. Going on a diet was only condoned as a health precaution but was condemned as an aesthetic measure. The spirit of the discussion of strong feelings expressed in uncompromising terms is probably more significant than its content. That could be construed not only in terms of the discourse, but possibly also as a caustic comment on the aesthetic value attributed to the elderly in our own culture (see, e.g., Featherstone & Hepworth 1990, 1991).

— "Did you see a programme last night on that immigration centre in Gambia?"

— "Yes, I saw most of it."

— "The Europeans involved in the Gambia crisis are people who deserve our respect far more than most of us."

— "Indeed, they do."

— "Yes. I was going to raise the point that where they can't help physically, many people who give a hand to those who are dying deserve nothing but respect."

— "That's why I find that the most obscene cult in our society is the cult of diet. I can't stand it personally, because I think it's offensive. It's offensive to our status as human beings in this world, and to deliberately curtail food consumption for aesthetic purposes—that doesn't make sense to me at all."

— "You mean, that we are vain."

— "I understand it, but the preoccupation with it, the obsession that people display about reducing food consumption, for whatever purpose—while half of the world is starving to death, I find it obscene, on moral grounds."

— "It seems to me that most of the preoccupations with weight in our society are disgusting. I, myself, cut down on butter for health reasons."

— "Yes, that's right, but I wasn't referring to any diet, I said specifically, for aesthetic . . . it's not even aesthetic grounds, it's for futile purposes, futile purposes."

— "Oh, yes, yes. There are no objections whatsoever to improving our fitness and our somatic adequacy or whatever you want to call it."

Past involvements, however, were adduced to give credence to personal commitment to social justice. At the same time the position of power and the hazards of misjudgement or abuse of authority had to be eliminated. The following recounts how one of the members was faced with the dilemma of power unaccompanied by acceptable criteria of selection and distribution. The action he took to resolve that predicament was to resign his post. This particular ending of that personal narrative is illuminating, since it marks the transition between the two identities—past career and present idealism. The very mention of the free decision taken by the member to relinquish a position of power and to incur loss of social status suggests that retirement was a voluntary act, not of shirking responsibility, but of assuming another one:

— "What's the criterion for a thing like that? And is it really a good thing for a vast quantity of money being amassed on one circumstance where there is another event elsewhere, Ethiopia or whatever?"

— "This is, of course, a lot of money, but at the same time there's another place in Africa where they are dying just as much."

— "It's very hard to select."

— "Yes, quite."

— "There's no general rule."

— "Yes, that's right."

— "Well, I heard some years ago—I was for a time a trustee of the Thalidomide Children's Trust, and that was a most extraordinary fact of 27 million pounds put into a trust fund."

— "There were, I believe, then, 300 children, but many of them have died since."

— "But what about all the other children with the same defects that have nothing to do with Thalidomide, because what Thalidomide did was to make a particular congenital aberration, and I really found it impossible to go on after a while."

— "Playing God."

Refusing to "play God" as a rationalization to retirement was at the same time an indictment of the professional ethics and social conduct of the whole of the medical establishment in which that member played an important part. Discreditation of social institutions on grounds of "hypocrisy," "abuse of power," or sheer mismanagement was common among the members and served to exonerate them from active involvement in the present and to discard the remnants of the past from their current identity. It also enabled members to distinguish clearly between the available and the desirable while ignoring the attainable. The world as they knew it was full of "defects" and deficiencies; the ideal universe of equality and justice they conjured up was a safe mental sanctuary. Retirement, which for most of the members was much more than just terminating professional life, was the rationale for not assuming any role in putting preaching into practice. This separation between word and action was a conscious state acknowledged by members, but not a cause for despair or remorse. Old age seemed to make allowances for this dual existence. The following demonstrates how medical hierarchy and its travesties, together with the alleged standard policies of the trade union, serve to comment on the state of the world and what could and ought to be done about it:

— "One of the most worrying things about our society at the present time is that we have had such advances, scientific in the broadest sense, that it is now possible to do the work that we need with roughly one eighth of the population unemployed. And the real problem in our society is to divide the work amongst eight eighths, not seven eighths, and that costs everybody something."

— "When you said that the Labour party has become a conservative party, it's the trade unions who have become the party who want all for the employed. And they're concerned about the unemployed. And let me tell you, we've got exactly the same situation in medicine, with the consultants saying their number should be increased and going home and making sure that it isn't, so that they have more junior doctors helping them without being given the opportunity of promotion. We have a kind of social injustice amongst this relatively well-to-do group. But it is quite as bad as anything the trade unions have done. It is very widespread, this defect in our society. It's a sort of thing Thatcher doesn't even think about."

— "But this is the sort of thing that a lot of us don't think about. I recall an article that I read about 12 years ago, concerning an inverted pyramid. What the argument boiled down to roughly was this: one consultant, when he got to the top, would have been working for 30 years, during which time 60 housemen, 15 registrars, 30 senior house officers, and possibly some senior registrars as well would have gone through his hands, all of whom were aspiring to become consultants themselves. How can that lot, which amounts to three figures, wait for one dead man's shoes? The pyramid should be the other way round."

— "Yeah, everybody has a chance to get on reasonably well, fall by the wayside, or change their minds, and that if one day—if one perhaps tried to structure society, as distinct from medicine, with that sort of philosophy in mind, much of these kinds of problems which were inherited from the first industrial Revolution, where nothing could possibly be eliminated, but shaped a working party that reported at the end of 1968 on this problem and provided the solution, and every four years since there's been another working party which has provided the same solution . . ."

[*Laughter*]

— "Then immediately the professional resistance in productions, by the time the four-year cycle has ended, the profession is screaming that the government hasn't done it. I think it really is devastating that a sought-after, highly educated sector of our population does this sort of thing—I tell you, they eat their young."

— "Well, the only hope is for alternative medicine to break it."

— "What you're saying is that the biggest enemy in Western society is personal greed."

— "Certainly."

— "I don't want to defend the trade unions, but why this particular thing on the lack of trade unions?"

— "I wonder if unions are like the others in that respect."

— "Yes, they find this a better way of doing things for themselves, but who thinks of doing it for everybody?"

— "Right. And, I mean, it's no virtue in us that we happen to think that way. It gives us a comfortable feeling. But, what the hell have we done about it?"

— "Hmm."

Hope, however, is not completely lost, for younger idealists do exist and some of them even have the clout to improve matters so that values of equality and humanism can be practiced. The following testifies to that encouraging possibility:

— "They are going to publish a lecture that a friend of mine, as good and younger than I am in general practice, gave at Harvard and, I forgot what he told me, but it is a wonderful presentation of what the physician ought to be trying to do in his society in the future. It was not a technical exposition. It was about the relationships with other people, because we are still less than happy about that dreadful tendency to know what's right for people, and see they do it. And it may not be right for that particular people. Those decisions require the participation of the people themselves, at least as much as of the technical expert. And it's patient participation that hasn't come forward nearly enough. In the States, where the thing is wholly commercial, you get it on a sort of commercial relationship, and that means the unfortunate patient just doesn't know— I mean—being exploited with technology. But in this country a relatively small part of people—only about two percent of all GP's who have a regular arrangement for communication with the population of their practices. Well, most doctors think in terms of 'it's my practice, and I run it my way.' But a practice is for the patient, and it isn't his practice, it's his invitation practice. I think that we're talking too much about medicine, but the same is true in social work—experts impose upon all the rest of society without having modification of what systems do to the people with whom it's going to be done."

Furthermore, better-informed patients and greater awareness of the mutual trust required in a doctor–patient relationship might move this process forward. The increasing number of malpractice suits attests to the emergence of a more balanced relationship between professional authority and clientele. These series of observations were the trigger for a significant discussion on the intricate relations between mastery of knowledge, social power and equality. The following discourse presents no exception to the usual pattern of the course of exchanges. It starts off with some comments on the medical profession and the patient's right to know and then proceeds to other remotely related concerns such as social work and eventually the operation of the classes at the U3A. What makes this particular discussion exceptional, however, is that it offers an interpretation of the key-concept guiding this chapter: equality. To put it succinctly, it is the transformation of any object of knowledge and authority into a subject with whom mutual relationship of an equal nature could be established. Patients, welfare cases, children, and elderly people are all examples for the authoritarian model of subject–object one-sided relationships. A reversal—or, as one member put it, "a modification"—of this model is the first principle or "the thing in itself" of equality. The ending of the discussion is an important testimony to the special relevance that such reversal bears for the members of the U3A. The direct implication is that since elderly people are out of bounds to authoritarian knowledge, they should not tolerate being objects for its agents:

— "The candidate is being interviewed by the appointing board, the appointing board is also being interviewed by the candidate—they have to show themselves, and in an exam the pupil is being examined, but so is his teacher."

— "Yes. The problems come from the fact that we think in terms of power hierarchy, rather than in terms of cooperation, and what happens is that what you have suggested—of transforming the object into a subject—is a very difficult process to contain by medical officers, social workers, whoever is in charge, because it curtails their authority—so they see it. What they don't understand is that at the end of the day they would be better informed and more efficient in their jobs because of it. But they feel threatened. They feel threatened because of another fact—because of the fact that more people in our society are better acquainted with all sorts of professions to pass judgement . . . to pass judgement and to be critical, even of a medical man, or the social worker, or anybody. And if I go to a doctor, I want to know everything there is to know about what's wrong with me. And I think that I have got a basic education to absorb and to understand it. And I was told by somebody—I don't know whether this is true or not, we've got a medical professional here to confirm it—that the worst patients for doctors are other doctors."

— "Yeah. It makes sense."

— "It makes the doctor, who is treating another doctor, much more vulnerable. And as a result his effort to reduce the patient into an object is much greater."

— "You know, we do learn to act in self-defence. Part of the general problem, I think, is that we have to conduct our lives in certain ways because you can't do something and start out from first principles every time. There are many things we have to decide, and when we have already decided, we have to go back and do some thinking again, because consequences of that kind are not everlasting, they are modified by changes in circumstances."

— "True. And I think what that really means is one question—and I speak again medically and I'm sure that it applies to any scientific research and probably the same in industry as well—which one should always be asking: Am I doing this because it's the routine, or am I doing it because it is going to contribute something to the public, or the job, or whatever I am going to do, or I don't do it?"

— "But if you keep asking yourself this sort of question, you will paralyse yourself completely, you won't be able to . . ."

— "Yes. Yes . . ."

— "And about 90 percent of what we do is routine. It's according to pre-scribed patterns or rituals or whatever you want to call them. And those very rare moments or reflexivity and of self-awareness happen only on the very rare occasion where you are confronted with a borderline situa-tion, which is neither here nor there, and it calls for our special attention, for our special consideration. I think if you as a doctor treat—I don't know—a hundred common colds a day, you won't stand to reflect upon them. But if you treat one symptom which is out of the ordinary, and which you would regard as puzzling, as perplexing, that will induce that moment that you are talking about."

— "If you have it this way, I suppose it really epitomizes the whole diffi-culty, because you start out thinking desperately about how you author-ize others who have been safe performers, but there you get to a point of expertise—and I think that it doesn't take very long until you suppress the actual thing that you have to do and subconsciously you do it, as you do in so many other cases."

— "You can't get back to the thing itself."

— "You certainly do."

— "Just sometimes you do, for example, you try to."

— "Yes, I—absolutely, I was just thinking about this. Yes. When I tried to teach my children table manners, they became aware of my own."

— "Yes, indeed."

— "Yes. Sure. That's why I will see to it that they never reach perfection."

— "That is a terrible thing, to show that the object of education always ought to be uneducated—always ought to be trying to make sure that the next generation is better than you are."

— "I think there is a weakness in our discussion as it is working out so far, that we have to overcome—and that is that we are too content with the teacher and his goals. But I think that in our age group and with our kind of make-up, there shouldn't be so much distinction as there needs to be in the ordinary teaching situation. And it ought to be more equal, I think, particularly with history things—I am not sure whether there are many subjects that by and large do not interest me."

— "That's correct."

— "Like the idea of the U3A."

— "We have a lot of courses."

— "Oh, yes, we do. But what I do think is that we are different from the younger age group. I mean, we are not learning from all that material by that kind of classroom teacher or tutor. I think we could certainly take a great deal of responsibility."

— "I don't think it's a question of the amount of time we've got. It's a question of instrumentality. And you don't learn for a degree you don't want to make use of."

— "That's it, yes."

CHAPTER 7

Reason:
"It's the Annihilation
of the World as We Know It"

Dismantling the rule of time and undoing social inequities were intellectual feats requiring a line of reasoning beyond common principles of chronology and hierarchy. The three preceding chapters illustrated how such reverse rules were systematically applied to a whole gamut of issues. This chapter is set to ascertain the core principles of those methods of reasoning.[1]

Central to this reasoning are concepts such as "first principles" and "the thing in itself." It should be noted, however, that I intend to analyse the use of those concepts and not their "meaning." This approach is based on two considerations—a methodological conviction and a theoretical postulate. From a methodological point of view, any meaning-seeking interpretation would seem prejudgemental, for it poses assumptions that cannot be proven within the framework of this study. (1) Should the source of "meaning" be sought beyond the situation of the group's activities, it might well be put out of bounds and become inaccessible. (2) Any reference to "meaning" presupposes interconnectedness of various existential universes. In other words, it is grounded in imagery, metaphor, and symbolic interaction.[2] One of the main findings of this research, however (see particularly chapter 6), shows a persistent attempt by members to introduce a new structural order into their existence by keeping divergent life-worlds apart.[3] In that respect, the pursuit of "meaning"—especially an overarching one—does not do methodological justice to the nature of the field. To quote Wittgenstein (1953:654) once again, it would be "a mistake to look for an explanation where we ought to look at what happens, that is, where we ought to have said: this language game is played."

From a theoretical standpoint, it would be self-defeating, if not self-subversive, to attribute interpretational values to a discourse whose primary purpose is to be rid of them. I regard this as a point of theory rather than methodology because I consider the utterances presented in this study as an articulated theory pertaining not only to the specific worlds of the people under study, but offering a set of propositions concerning major issues of conceptual thinking. It behoves a researcher to strive for an optimum of congruence between his or her theoretical frames and those of the subjects whom he or she seeks to understand (cf. Fabian 1983), and more so perhaps in a case such as this, where the language of research ("-etics") is congenital with the language of the actors ("-emics").[4] The latter, in our case, tried to embark on a journey to the "real thing" or to "first principles" whose essence is lack of conceptual and interpretative concomitants. The language of things-in-themselves and first principles is a literal and metonymical language and therefore cannot be approached with metaphorical vehicles of meaning linking it to anthropological discourse, or any other universe of discourse, for that matter. There is no signifier for such a language in anthropological language; it must be its own signifier. However, a comparison of the system of thought of the elderly with other, parallel philosophical endeavours (such as those of Plato and Goethe, for instance) will be pursued in the last chapter.

It is, therefore, my conviction that the language reflecting such formulations must abide by its own rules. It would seem that conventional symbolic anthropology does not offer such a way of translation, and, with the exception of some schools of thought,[5] it is designed to serve the understanding of a holistic context, thus steering the researcher to destinations against the current of the rationale of this study. So, let the people under study stand at the helm of their own intellectual ship.

A subject that has already been mentioned several times could offer a gambit for the ensuing discussion. This is the question of trust and its origins. The collapse of many other systems of mutual obligations and social reliance left trust as one of the last citadels of support. It is hardly surprising that this fragile subject received a great deal of attention by members. The explanation that a relationship of trust is based on either deference to authority or mutual negotiated interest did not satisfy members. Both bases seemed ephemeral and shaky. Rather, it was suggested that "like in primitive societies, trust comes before action." Viewing trust as "first principle," the antecedent of social cooperation, has two significant implications: (1) It provides an unconditional security of a taken-for-granted human asset; (2) it implies a complete separation between the "principle" and its applications or "meanings." Indeed, it was maintained that modern society corrupted this original and pure form of trust and converted it into its opposite—a labile, uncertain, and treacherous conception.

For the members, "trust" in itself was in fact not an explanation, and that vein of thinking, indeed, guided much of the deliberations. Facts were not conceived of as tangible real objects, but as the root of the matter discussed. The reluctance to avail themselves of conceptual reading was thus construed as an expression of "not wanting explanations but facts."

The separation of fact from explanation produced some interesting observations which otherwise might have been interpreted as self-contradictory. Hence, for example, members vehemently voiced their objection to prejudice, not for being untrue, but for being presented as if it were not reality. In other words, they accepted any view of the other as long as that view was the thing itself and not its interpretation. Prejudice was thus described as the conceptions of others and therefore illegitimate devices for constructing the world. Illuminating illustrations for this reasoning were competitiveness among Jews, which was regarded as a "real trait," and the "smell of Indians, which is the irremovable odour of curry powder." It inevitably followed that feelings induced by prejudice did not prevail in this frame of reference, since facts are neutral. That was another corroboration of the non-relativistic view engendered in the group, shaping a predominant feature of its discourse. It may be termed "the non-phenomenological law," which rules out the possibility of phenomenon-based inference of facts. To phrase it in less formal language, it could follow the rule of thumb that appearances are not to be trusted to produce evidence regarding first principles. Members, however, stated the case in a clearer fashion:

— "I think that people believe that what you say is the way that you say it, and what you do is the way that you do it. Could I suggest that possibly this concept is false?"

— "Yes, all right, because we got our relationships according to fronts, we respond to fronts, we don't respond to inner values, we don't respond to inherent properties of personality, or what the person really is. Because, on the basis of the flimsy evidence obtained by communicating with other people, we can't behave otherwise, mainly because most of the people we encounter during our life are casual acquaintances. They are not beings developing intimate relationships. The tragedy is that even with those we do have intimate relations with, sometimes we have the feeling that we don't know them. And this is really the tragic thing. It's not that you don't—that I don't know you and you don't know me, because our ways will part, but the people we are committed to spend most of our lives with sometimes—we have the terrible feeling that they are really strangers. And this is wrong."

— "I think it's the advantage, the complexity of human nature."

— "Advantage, it is. Yes."

Estrangement is, therefore, connected to our inability to know the other and to the socially erected barriers of façade fencing off one subject from another. In a discussion about relationships between parents and children it was suggested that what drives children out of their homes, makes them rebel against their parents, and pushes them towards alternative identities is not a lack of investment on the part of the parents, but the fundamental absence of love. This absence cannot be accounted for by the relative weight of parental resources bestowed upon a child, but it is an expression of the necessary emotional bonding between people. "Either you have got it or you haven't, and in any event you can't do anything about it," asserted one of the members, and another went so far as to say that one should distinguish between the availability of love in a relationship and the relationship itself. When asked to elaborate on this unclear observation, he maintained that love is not contingent upon its subject, and "if one of my children were to die, it wouldn't change my feelings towards him, and if I did not love him before, I would not love him after." Love, therefore, is another example of "a thing in itself" divorced from relationships or persons, and not amenable to fostering, cultivating, or causing to vanish. In fact, throughout the whole course of discussions, which covered a period of nearly a year and a half, precious little was mentioned regarding kith and kin. Children were ignored, and marital relationships were overlooked. On one occasion, when the world of gardening and flower-growing was discussed, some members who happened to carry photographs of their own houses and gardens produced them to compare notes. Some of the pictures showed other persons, presumably related to members. Not a single comment was passed as to the nature of their presence in the photos, and no courtesy explanation was offered as to their identities. On the very rare occasion when family members were invoked, it was by way of abstract reference, to make a point of argument. In all such situations, names, status, or other identifying social or personal insignia were not volunteered.

Like previously discussed observations as to the social character of the educational system and particularly that of boarding-schools, the upbringing of children was not treated as a product of family relationship, nor was it seen as a haphazard fact. Rather, it was perceived to be a direct consequence of the working of the social system, which "does not allow children to learn anything about themselves and the world, but forces them to be its own image."

Socialization in general and learning in particular were conceived of as a pre-programmed conditioning blocking self-awareness. These assumptions were connected to one of the most disturbing subjects that members pondered upon: the question of being inhuman. Genetic explanations, some of which, previously stated, did not satisfy members, and the view of the social repression of self-consciousness, appeared more convincing.

Unlike common processes of learning when subjects–students are trained and conditioned to become part of the studied object or to "absorb" it, their own feat, as seen by members, was to create a cleavage between subject and object, essence and phenomenon. In a sense, it could be construed as a method of undoing and deconceptualization.

This postulate, when drawn to its logical conclusion, dismisses the connection between cause and effect and formulates a type of reasoning free of causality, consisting within a cycle of an eternal return (to first principles) rather than of a linear chain of progressive knowledge. One of the self-evident implications of such an approach is the shedding of responsibility for one's actions and the adoption of a fatalistic view of interrelatedness. A discussion concerning juvenile delinquency might demonstrate how this conception is applied to education and to the connection between cause and effect. Having recounted several media-reported violent assaults by youths on elderly persons, members brought up the possibility of corrective programmes. After a member remarked that "one of them could be my grandson," the discussion took a definite direction of ruling out any possibility of rehabilitation:

— "That doesn't make any sense whatsoever—I mean, there is no rationale behind it, to justify any expected consequences. And what do you achieve by it? On the contrary, it will only develop a greater sense of self-discipline in these people, that's all—which will be very conducive in their illegal pursuits."

This wonderment about human nature became the subject of a heated discussion following the Bradford fire—a fire that broke out in a football stadium and claimed a large number of casualties, including many fatalities. The televised scenes from this arena showed horrific pictures of persons being burnt alive while the spectators opposite were cheering and jeering. It was the only discussion that was charged with high emotional tones, not only because of the tremendous impact of the event and its moral implications, but also owing to the critical questions it evoked. Was it a representational display contrived and concocted by the mass media?

Or, to formulate it in our terms—was it just an appearance, or was it the real thing, a hair-raising demonstration of the essence of the human character? The choice to be made was between a spectacle of dehumanization or an unadulterated true dehumanization. It was also a choice between the representational phenomenon and the comfortable solution of imagery rather than reality. However, in line with their insistence on equality as the "real thing," we would expect that members advocate, in the case of the Bradford fire and its implications of human cruelty, the spectacular rather than the essential.

— "Jumping and hopping and chanting."

— "Some kind of orgy."

— "It was, well, yes and no. I mean—the image that it conjured up in my mind was the Inquisition time."

— "Yes. Was it a hysteria?"

— "I don't know. I'm not sure."

— "You see them jumping up and down out of joy—I mean."

— "Yes, but it was really all part of the sheer incredibility, wasn't it? Of those witnessing and those even taking part. But it just wasn't a real thing, at all, I mean that—I'm sure that it—they hadn't grasped what was going on."

— "Well, some of them had grasped it."

— "I mean, it was a colourful, exciting spectacle to them at that moment."

— "Yes."

— "I think they would see differently when they knew there would be suffering and death."

— "Well, actually . . ."

— "But they didn't treat it in terms of death or suffering. They treated it in term of—it's not just a spectacle, but beating the enemy, I think. It was beating the enemy, because it doesn't matter what happens to the enemy. It was one of the most ultimate examples of dehumanization that I can recall. I mean, just reducing the people to their role as the other camp."

— "I really would hesitate to accept that interpretation of something that I didn't witness close up. I just do not believe that there could have been a crowd there applauding the burning of persons."

— "I saw those few shots, and there weren't people jumping up and down."

— "Yes. But what were they doing?"

— "I'm sure they were aware."

— "Now, depending on your circumstances and the time of reaction and so on, you interpret it seriously or not. If you've been in a car accident or people who've been badly injured, at first they're not aware of it. So is this business of—even if someone were jumping up and down with joy, it was because it wasn't registering with those people."

— "And why not? It's just a fire—why shouldn't they react immediately?"

— "I mean, they saw."

— "Not only this. We saw on the television that person who escaped from the stand with his hair and body and clothes all on fire, and the crowd was watching and jumping up and down, cheering."

— "I think that there were people who were leaping on him and trying to put it out."

— "I'm talking about one section of the spectators."

— "Have you any idea what it's like with a big fire, with the amount of heat that would be projected across that ground? The people on the other side of the ground would be getting an amount of heat that'd be barely tolerable."

— "But anyway, what you saw was a picture—flat and two-dimensional."

— "Right."

— "In which a number of things were put together. If you were there, with the different spaces between the different things."

— "And the other thing that I would like to remind you of is that once upon a time there used to be some people torn to pieces by lions in a very similar exhibition."

— "But that is exactly the kind of analogy which I want to prove."

— "Well, I don't think that's a fair analogy at all. The thing I saw and particularly remember was men—many of them policemen—pulling out people and putting out flames."

— "What is interesting is the actual presentation of the facts."

— "I remember from the newsreel tape—I think it took about four minutes or five for the thing to take a grip, and then it roared away."

— "And certainly earlier on—I remember certainly—a crowd of young people laughing and the—after that in my own memory is that wonderful moving scene with a fellow coming on to the pitch and the policeman covering him over."

— "Yes."

— "But the interesting thing is there—you see—you remember these stories and recollect them in different ways."

— "This is where the historian comes in—he edits them and makes any point he wants to raise."

— "This is the famous story of Rashomon—you know, the Japanese tale. A group of people witnessed a rape, and every one of them has a different, an entirely different interpretation of it. And they are all right. They are all correct."

— "Well, look, I do think in your interpretation of that event you are aware of the effect of heat coming from that fire, which would have come right across the pitch. I mean, I don't say this from personal observation, but one of my jobs was to be chief medical officer to the Home Office, and I happened to be responsible for an inquiry into the medical conditions of fire, and there was a lot of evidence about what happens in really big fires before a committee I was chairing then. And I would deduce from that, that the blast of heat that was coming across the pitch there would be beyond understanding to the people on the other side. And I do remember what seems to be incredible—the bravery and endurance of people who went back into that heat."

— "Yes."

— "That's the one which sticks in my mind."

— "Well, here again I'd say this from personal experience of being involved in a fire. You see, to the real degree—I say, in fairness, your mental faculties act in such a way so that you go in because you know that you need to rescue a person. I was saying and . . ."

— "On the other hand, we know quite well that in a state of ecstasy people are immune, people are impervious to the messages registered by their senses."

— "But you can't be impervious to really hot air going into your lungs, which will kill you quickly."

— "Well, yes, but I mean that this is the extreme end of the ladder."

— "Yes."

— "Not at the extreme end, I—really—I wonder if you know what a big fire does."

— "Try going into a room where a fire is hitting the ceiling. And that was just an example. And to say that I couldn't because it was getting bigger and bigger, nevertheless, I was trying to pull out a person from there— and at the time I wasn't thinking about the fact that I was burning, singeing, and so on."

— "Also, we have to take into account that the information on which we are basing this discussion is television information. I mean, the picture that we saw was edited for us, was directed for us, was composed for us by the television crew."

— "Yes."

— "And this is not reality."

This discussion confronted members not only with moral and intellectual dilemmas, but also, by the very nature of its context, with the issue of death. While humanism acquired the unequivocal and unanimous status of "the thing in itself," death was treated as its complete opposite—utter nothingness, a conceptual as well as substantive void. The issue of handling death is presented at some length in part III. For our present purposes, suffice it to locate it as part of the overall discourse. As stated in structural terms, death was the other pole of the "real thing." In existential terms, however, the avoidance of the subject was tantamount to denying it, and when forced to relate to it, members attached to it all the counter-properties characterizing the "thing in itself." Attitudes towards death were culturally conditioned and hence represented the ultimate in relativity. In fact, the diverse range of funerary rites and bereavement patterns was introduced as the only phenomenon distinguishing different societies:

— "When life was a matter of 25 years, if you were lucky, then it was not such an event—that it ended—and the really very matter-of-fact way in which reference is made on the death of prominent figures in the Anglo-Saxon chronicles, who have none of the tearing of hair and weeping and so on that you will get now. This is quite in contrast to the present attitude."

The closer members approached the subject of the attitude towards death in their own society, the more cynical and overtly critical their views became. They posited some of the most practical positions along the course of the discourses and even discredited any custom connected with the sacredness of or the respect given to the dead and to the unborn—both regarded as non-living entities.

— "But what about the sort of nonsense that is going on at the present time over abortion or contraception or whatever. And—in which all sorts of people like Enoch Powell are ready to decide what young women should do."

— "Yes, but this is a very interesting point, because what we see here is people trying to hold on to fragments of moral order in a desperate attempt to preserve something which has already passed—which has already gone. And the public responds that way."

— "Yes, but . . ."

— "That is the despairing aspects of it—the public response. Because the public is in the same situation."

— "What we are witnessing now is really a case of symbols and myths in reality. And this is a very sad state of affairs. It's nothing new, I know, but we've had them in abundance lately, that's the problem, we've had too much of it. When sometimes years pass and you don't encounter such things and then—here we have it condensed within one or two months."

— "I wonder whether . . ."

— "So often in these questions we are seeing gut reactions when we ought to be seeing people. Ask, what is in the interests of the people most concerned?"

— "Well, the example of abortion and contraception and so on and so forth. Or, for that matter, if you like, Prince Charles and Princess Diana going to Mass at the same time when the bishop visits Northern Ireland."

This stance did not stop at abortion and still-born babies but was logically extended to their own lives. Euthanasia was regarded as a legitimate prerogative, and prolonging life by artificial means was condemned as a form of perversion.

— "I'm not sure what our attitude is now, because I think it's rapidly changing from one with considerable concern to considerable indifference again."

— "But in our own culture, we are all deeply upset when we hear about the death of young people."

— "Yes."

— "I recently had the misfortune to have to go to a couple of funerals of young people who had died under difficult circumstances, and it was frightfully upsetting because it's not part of one's—one doesn't expect it."

— "The B.M.A.'s sent me books about bereavement to review—and some of them are almost unbelievable. There are experts on bereavement who tell you how to work it all out, and it takes so long and then everything is all right."

— "Have they ever lost a child?"

— "I think they'll never be the same again after that."

— "We can have a tremendously involved evolution of law, much of which is empty talk. And alongside it, we get almost absurdities like putting mechanical hearts into people at the end of their lives to postpone their deaths by days or weeks. What kind of progress is that?"

— "I mean, quality of life is a kind of a dominant issue. But we—that business of artificial heart and that sort of thing—is nearly in a momentum of that technology. You see, the person who is inventing it is not thinking about prolonging somebody's life, but about making it."

— "It is like solving a difficult problem cleverly."

— "Probably. Now, the consequences of that, of course, are very often extremely dubious."

— "But the operative word there is "clever" rather than "thought," and much of this is a perverse pride."

— "I agree."

— "That's what most English people think. Not the consideration that they are giving a patient or victim or whatever, you see, something that they want."

Religious solace was not expressly sought, and faith was described by one of the members as a form of "cosiness" associated with false security that serves the interests of maintaining social order. The production of the striving for "cosiness" was depicted as one of modern society's consumer items which has become an unreachable myth. As one of the members put it: "The tragedy of our society is that cosiness has become a commercial myth. You can't naturally incorporate it into our daily life anymore." Cosiness did occupy a real location where it could be found, not as a social counterfeit, but as an authentic reality. That was the sense of belonging to a small informal community, governed by primary relationships of trust and mutual care. Such experiences, based mainly on childhood in small villages or close-knit urban families, were recalled with longing and tenderness. When this bout of nostalgia was too much to bear, members reverted to the manufacturer of representations—television—and explained the success of soap operas and serial dramas as a reflection of the yearning of people to reach that "real cosiness of continuity and belonging." They also maintained, however, that this objective could not be attained through social prestige and position of authority. A member observed that "even though belonging to a social class is at the heart of our system, it does not mean a thing as far as the essence of our being is concerned. I was born to one class, married into another, my profession placed me in yet another class, and my children seem to identify themselves with different classes. Still, that does not make any difference to who I really am."

The quest for first principles and things-in-themselves spells a unique reconstruction of a world of meaning practised through a deconstruction of the actual world of appearances. A member once commented on the implications of these discourses to the overall world-view of the members by posing the following question: "Is it the annihilation of the world as we know it, or a mechanism to safeguard what is left and redefine the world?" This recurrent existential pragmatism does shed a light on the place of the studied texts within the overall context of members' participation in the U3A. We have observed the collapse of time, the dismantling of social space, and the dissolution of conventional reasoning. All these processes happened because of the irrelevance of pre-old-age conceptions of time, space, and reason to the lives of the elderly. Hence, surrogate worlds could emerge as alternatives to those that were demolished.

If this assumption is tenable, then the behavioural context of the other activities of members within the setting of their organization ought to corroborate it. In other words, the mode of articulation dominating the texts should also be regarded as a context-structuring device, substituting those more traditional context-structuring devices previously forfeited. It should thus be predicted that instead of chronological time of inevitable decline, a new recursive non-linear temporal universe will emerge. The lost horizons of object-oriented society could be replaced by an alternative reflexive system of boundary delineation and maintenance. The collapse of reason associated with loss of status, diminishing involvement, and increased dependency is substituted by an autonomous, self-contained social sanctity of one's peers. The last section of the book will present a series of case studies to demonstrate how the U3A became an arena where those three transformations took place. In describing these transformations, we turn from the texts to the context, while portraying the ways by which the rules of the former determine the meaning of the latter. Re-embracing the vital connection of text and context, the linguistic forms traced in the texts under investigation become again modes of articulation.

This threefold manifestation of constructing context was not coincidental, and our contention is that its understanding must draw on the properties of discourse encoded in the textual presentations hitherto unfolded. The argument expounded upon in the next three chapters is that the behavioural patterns to be described are generated by the interface between the two types of languages underpinning communication among members: the language of "real things" and ideal forms, and the language of the practical, the changing, and the adaptive. In the course of the discussions, which were conducted in the safe arena of the non-committal, undisturbed atmosphere of a debating society, members were able to split the two languages and to keep apart talk about the existential from talk about existence. On certain occasions, as we have learnt, the two were inadvertently intermingled and had to be disentangled. Outside the confines of the "cosiness" of the discussion-room things were evidently different. The organization offered a self-sponsored framework for action, but not the content and substance to fill it with. That was the daily undertaking of members who created the manner and dynamics by which various activities were thought out, performed, and changed. That was, as we shall see, a precarious process of trial and error and, sometimes, stretching intentions to the limit of their feasibility. But, as suggested, this was not a haphazard exercise in gaining more ground for activity just for the sake of it. Rather, in the terms proposed in this book, it was an application of the language and the vast experience of the practice to serve and furnish the language of the fundamental and the "thing in itself." This was carried out by constructing a field of action where boundaries, shared behaviour, and mutually reinforced pursuits could be established to maintain the desirable and to ward off the threatening.

If the abstract notion of context is to be practically understood as generally emerging, in a distinct spatio-temporal setting, from the interplay between two sets of factors—synthetically defined as determinacy and indeterminacy (cf. Moore 1978), constant and variant—it is suggested that in the life of elderly people, the latter might pose a serious threat to the former. Hence, when settings for the aged are designed and constructed by the old, it is reasonable to expect them to reflect that state, namely that an attempt is made to tilt the balance between the uncontrollable and the controllable, towards the latter. The following case studies of the construction of an old-age peer-group context subscribe to this principle by harnessing the power of pragmatic action to the exigencies of transfixing a world based on resistance to what is so deeply embedded in this practical approach—change and unpredictability.

The three concrete phenomena with which members had to contend to sustain a manageable order were impending death, the negative cultural imagery of the old, and the ominous loss of autonomy. These were all private but nevertheless salient manifestations of the all-embracing issues of time, space, and reason. The case studies to follow unravel the efforts invested in containing each of these hazards, framing it within the safeguarded context of the U3A.

PART III

CONTEXT:
TESTING OUT FOR AGEING

The soul is like an eye: when resting upon that on which truth and being shines, the soul perceives and understands, and is radiant with intelligence; but when turned towards the twilight of becoming and perishing, then she has opinion only, and goes blinking about, and is first of one opinion and then of another, and seems to have no intelligence. . . . Like ourselves, strange prisoners who see only their own shadows, or the shadows of one another, which the fire throws on the opposite wall of the cave.

[from Plato's Republic]

CHAPTER 8

Time Recaptured:
The Hidden Agenda of Death

Rarely raised during discussions, treatment of the subject of death was confined to its practical aspects, and its relation to the essence of life was completely denied. In other encounters and gatherings of the U3A, where systematic deliberations did not constitute the proper style of discussion, sarcasm was used in conjunction with this subject. While making arrangements for their annual Christmas dinner, members attending the general meeting of the organization commented: "I hope that Christmas dinner next year won't come too quickly," or "I will do it next year, too, if I am still alive." Self-mockery apart, the commonplace attitude towards death was of avoidance, to the extent that, following a coroner's lecture on "Murders in and around Cambridge," the U3A audience did not use question time to address the subject of crime against the elderly or death of elderly people by misadventure. All their questions concerned non-age-related fatalities, except for the avid interest some of them expressed in the mysterious causes of cot-death. That could be attributed either to their roles as grandparents or to the implication inherent in the phenomenon of sudden unpredictable death.

This attitude of denial had a dramatic effect when a rumour, which was subsequently confirmed to be true, spread that during one of the U3A parties one of the participants had suffered a heart-attack and died on the premises. Other members, who attended to him just before his death, left the body upstairs and, not letting anybody else into the secret, allowed the party to continue uninterrupted. Regardless of the faithfulness of this description to the actual facts as they happened, the message of this local narrative was clear—death was not to be part of the U3A. In fact, the U3A's reason for existence was in its power to provide collective means to banish death from its midst.

Refraining from death-related topics was a manageable linguistic exercise, and, indeed, members, while talking freely about belonging to the category of the old, rarely associated it with passing away. However, the stark fact that in our society the occurrence of death is most frequent among the aged could not be overlooked by members, and barriers between themselves at present and their inevitable future finitude had to be erected. The building bricks with which such walls were erected were other elderly people—mainly those who, for reasons of severe physical or mental disability, could not be counted as possible candidates for the U3A.

The case of the physically handicapped was the most difficult to handle, since no suggestion was made as to their unsuitability to join the organization. Quite the reverse—in all meetings ample lip-service was given to the commitment of the U3A to include and encourage the disabled to join its ranks. However, intentions and plans to facilitate such inclusion were hampered by lack of cooperation from members. In spite of pleas to members to give a helping hand in assisting the disabled, very few volunteered to undertake such practical tasks. It is interesting to note that on many occasions the proverbial justification for such calls for help was that "charity begins at home"—"home" being the state of being old, and "charity" an act of splicing it up into sub-categories according to physical fitness.

Administering "charity" to other elderly persons seemed to be less complicated in the case of those whose condition could not possibly place them on the same level as the members of U3A. There were inmates of nursing homes and other geriatric institutions whose active involvement with the outside world was extremely restricted and, in most cases, amounted only to visitors and exposure to the mass media. Extending help to them would have been a reflection of the gap between the two categories of old people. Such help, however, was not forthcoming, despite attempts made by some members in support of such action. The other elderly, namely the "fourth age," were nevertheless used to fulfil the role of being a curtain between "normal" ("third") old age, and death.

The U3A had a research committee, which carried out a number of projects, a few of which are the subject of the following discussion. The

U3A itself was portrayed by Professor Peter Laslett, its founder and head, who also chaired the committee:

> On 21st. July 1981, in the Guildhall at Cambridge, we adopted the word "University" at the first meeting of what was to become The University of the Third Age, because it seemed the proper description of our intentions. From the outset, however, we have recognized that we could defend this title only if our institution did what it could to add to knowledge, as universities do. By this we meant knowledge in general, of any kind, such knowledge as with our resources we could recover or help to recover. The knowledge we are particularly after, however, is knowledge of ourselves, as those in the Third Age, of our place in the society to which we belong, and of the situation of that society as a whole in respect of age, ageing and ageism. We want to be as helpful as we can to those in the Third Age, in intellectual and in practical matters too. [Lambert, Laslett, & Clay 1984, Foreword]

The pursuit of self-knowledge was a double-edged prong, since it enabled members to formulate and disseminate their own views of themselves without the supposed prejudice of the non-old (see chapter 9 for a detailed discussion of this point), and at the same time it drove them into areas of undesirable knowledge, such as death. The two case studies to be described, particularly the second one, demonstrate this danger.

Some members of the research committee, whose total membership at the time of the research was 16, were non-elderly professionals whose interests and sympathies urged them to contribute their knowledge to the benefit of the committee. Such a person was a geriatrician who solicited the help of the committee in studying the situation of television viewing in geriatric institutions vis-à-vis the wishes of inmates and their expressed preferences. Conceived of as almost the only link with the outside world, it was the objective of the doctor to enhance and improve it for the benefit of patients as well as for the convenience of personnel.

The initial response of the committee was of keen support, and, having been debriefed by the doctor on some preliminary findings that he produced, the committee pledged their assistance in carrying out the project. For that purpose, two questionnaires were devised, one to ascertain the condition of television viewing in the institution and the other to glean inmates' views and wishes on the matter. Following that, a call for volunteer researchers to be recruited from the members of the U3A was issued by the committee.

The tacit assumption of the researchers was twofold. It supposed television viewing in geriatric institutions to be a non-voluntary act greatly dominated and dictated by members of staff, but at the same time of no real importance to patients who had lost interest in life and lacked the capacity to control it. This assumption was partly confirmed by the initial information obtained by the doctor, and this could account for both the verbal consent to take part in the research and the phrasing of some of the questions:

- "If you don't watch, why not?"
- "If you do watch, why?" (e.g. pleasure, information, to kill time)
- "Who decides if and when it should be switched on/off?"
- "Who decides the volume?"
- "Who decides the programme?"
- "Is your enjoyment impaired by difficulties of vision or hearing?"

This sub-category of decrepit elderly was assigned properties of another breed of objects rather than fellow-subjects. This is borne out by the high degree of dependency on others to which they were deemed to be fecklessly subjected, by making them into a research object and resource of knowledge concerning institutional life rather than the state of being old, and by labelling them as a distinctly different type of elderly people who are at the "fourth age." This last form of branding placed the institutionalized and the socially dependent as a human buffer zone distancing the active, alert, and self-sufficient from close proximity to imminent death. The "fourth age" was, hence, regarded as completely separate and distinct. The very properties which (in the eyes of "third-age" elderly) disqualified it from being included in the "normal" social circle qualified its antithesis—the third age—to become part of a progressive life course. Transitions from the third to the fourth age were never discussed.

The reluctance to cross these invisible but nevertheless rigid borders was obliquely expressed in the very poor response to the call for support to this research project. The research coordinators anticipated as much, and hence restricted themselves to expect a modest positive recruitment: "Even if only 10 institutions are visited, and 10 residents interviewed, that would still give a sample of 100. One hopes, of course, for a larger army of volunteers, but the response is very difficult to predict," stated a letter issued by the committee in an attempt to promote the study. The number of volunteers was well below even this minimum, and the project had to be abandoned.

Constructing the life cycle as a divisible sequence of discrete states rather than of continuous duration[1] was compatible with the view propounded in the discussion group (see previous chapters) that events are segmentary units unconnected by natural development or inherent continuity. This model of unchangeability enabled members to treat life stages as if they were separate from each other, to forestall the future, and to avoid personal references to death. Instead, when the eventuality of death was mentioned, it was phrased in terms of a universal, aphoristic adage such as "we are all going to die one day" or "nobody lives for ever." The obliteration of any association with the near-death category of the "fourth age" was buttressed by encouraging members to take up "life member- ship" of the U3A, thereby denying the plausibility of disengagement from the present stage.

Transforming the organization into a safe enclave containing the present members' lives spelt not only obviating the future, but also, as an empirical and logical conclusion, a dismissal of the past. It was already indicated that members were not inclined to boast about their past careers, or to use them as vital assets to advance their position in the organization. However, even as an object for research, the past was not considered to be a subject of high priority, or even worthy of academic pursuit. Moreover, the very emphasis on equality demanded that past careers, achievements, and credits, as well as any other measures of possible contrast and conflict, would be abandoned in favour of members' avowed egalitarianism.

This attitude was thrown into relief when two members approached the research committee with a request to be assisted and sponsored in record- ing the "local cultural heritage of the countryside around Cambridge." They explained their wish to engage in this research by the desire "to preserve local oral history." Members of the research committee, like most members of the U3A, usually showed keen interest in promoting courses concerning English history and, particularly, that of the Cambridge region. However, as we shall discover in the final chapter analysing the curricu- lum of the U3A, the near-past was of no interest to members. The commit- tee followed this line and, giving short shrift to the proposed project, discounted it as "an amateurish exercise in oral history." The promoters were said to have "only one research asset—spontaneity," which was a "non-starter" for pursuing a serious project deserving support. A further informal discussion revealed that it was not the research competence nec- essary for implementing the proposal that bothered members, but, rather, its implications. Members rejected the idea of uncovering immediate past history and maintained that "we do not want to reflect on past histories."[2] This stance was no exception to the rules established in the discussion group, and it was anchored in the conviction that the fragmentation of time—past, present, and future—could avert the inevitable interlinkage leading to death.

Notwithstanding the many manifestations of death-avoidance, the sub- ject of terminality reemerged in various forms, and members' incessant efforts to eschew it did not keep up with its recurrence in their U3A life.

The subject surfaced on numerous occasions and was usually fobbed off or hustled off. However, when the preoccupation with death was in the guise of practical reasoning, and the subject was presented as a service to members, it became enmeshed in the metaphoric language of pragmatism.

The mixing of the two separate codes—the literal and the metaphoric—produced an intolerable situation for members, and the resulting mess, jeopardizing the accomplishment of a dual referential scope, had to be disentangled. Such a set of circumstances emerged subsequent to a proposition made by some members to respond to what they considered to be the plight of many of their peers and to investigate the cost of arranging and conducting a funeral. It transpired that many members became involved in the unpalatable business of seeing to the burial ceremonies of friends and relatives, and that for several of them it turned out to be a most unpleasant experience. With great trepidation and apprehension, a decision was taken at the research committee to empower a sub-committee to undertake the project. The project never came to fruition, and, in spite of the considerable amount of time and other resources invested in it, it was bound to terminate—or, as one of the members put it, "to be buried." That resolution was tersely phrased, stating: "Agreed to discontinue the project on 'Funeral Arrangements and Costs' because members had lost interest in the project." That was the end of a rather long saga involving some dramatic moments, which eventually led to the realization that standing at the brink of death, even with the protection of the safety-net of doing research, was too much to bear.

Being highly conscious of the very sensitive nature of the study they were embarking on, members prepared a two-step design involving a pilot survey to develop tools for devising the main line of inquiry. This stage, however, was not to be reached. Following is a brief history of the rise and fall of the "Funeral Arrangements and Costs" project.

Two types of questionnaires were personally distributed among members, the first to persons who had had some experience in arranging a funeral and the second to persons without such experience. The first questionnaire was intended to examine the experience-based views of those who were at one time or another responsible for arranging a funeral. The second questionnaire scanned attitudes towards the subject expressed by people with no such experience. Response was fairly good, and there was no question of refusal to cooperate with the researchers. The answers, however, seemed to touch upon points the coordinators of the study had not bargained for. A cursory scan of some of the preliminary data gathered during the pilot stage of the research might demonstrate the extent of the unravelling of the hidden agenda of death that was made explicit in the survey.

It is important to note that with the target population of the study being the membership of the U3A, the age of most respondents—namely 22 out of 32—was over 60, the remainder being between the ages of 40 and 59. This in itself strengthened the identification of the research committee with the human source of the information obtained.

In addition, the range of occupations held by respondents—science, medicine, education, welfare, civil service, and the arts—contributed to placing respondents on a par with members of the committee. A final point of basic statistics is the age group to which the deceased persons belonged. The great majority occupied the age bracket between 70 and 89, which, particularly in its bottom section, corresponded to the ages of members.

The implications of these figures were not overlooked, but they were not sufficient to produce the kind of reaction that eventually closed the project. A step in that direction was the various comments and observations made in the course of the interviews, which could be described as narratives of "death review." The eventuality of sudden death was such a landmark: "The arrangements were not as easy as if we were living in the same town. The death occurred suddenly in London, we were contacted by the police and asked to contact the coroner. We travelled to London immediately to find that a post-mortem had been carried out. We were able to arrange everything on the same day. We had great help from the coroner and the police." The abruptness of the situation is accompanied by having no control over it, depending entirely on decisions made by official bodies.

Another practical aspect of looking at the stark facts of death through the screen of reporting funeral arrangements was the mention of the dead body. The following recollection couples it with other distasteful experiences: "I had selected a certain funeral director, but found that he was cheating me. It seems that the cost of transporting the body from the home to the hospital for post-mortem was paid by the Public Health Department." Or another critical remark: "The nursing home wished for quick removal of the deceased." Relating to body-disposal procedures such as cremation and types of coffins amplified the presence of the corpse in those reports. Rumours about the treatment of the body upon preparing it for burial drew members closer to the scene behind choral and floral. "Neighbours informed me that rings, including wedding rings, are often removed by the funeral director, who then keeps them."

Those grim assertions did not influence much the overall impression of respondents that their treatment by funeral directors was fair and compassionate: "It was arranged with kindness and respect for our family feelings and carried out with great dignity"; "In painful circumstances all practical matters were carried out smoothly." There was even a description of a pleasant ceremony: "Our mother had lived a good, useful, and happy life. We tried to arrange a cheerful service of thanksgiving, with good singing and music (led by five strapping grandsons). The funeral was a happy occasion, a fitting farewell to a beloved mother and grandmother." The research coordinator made a special point of adding a comment specifying the extreme old age of the deceased, implying that that kind of death does not belong to the category of the third age.

An ominous sign that the investigation was heavily fraught with insufferable tension was the resignation of a member of the team following a death in his own family. The final straw, however, which dissolved the project, was a special meeting of the research committee to which a research student conducting an anthropological study on the world of undertakers was invited by the committee to give a talk about her observations. The decision to enter the very heart of burial preparations was not welcomed by all, but it was thought that breadth and depth of background knowledge must be gained if the research subject was to be treated seriously. The student captured the sombre attention of her audience for an hour and a half, after which no questions were asked nor any comments made. The main theme of the talk was the abuse of corpses by those involved in handling them. The research was an ethnographic account and as such provided ample first-hand gruesome details as evidence to support its claim.

After the student had left, some members expressed their dismay at the findings of the report, and a few admitted to being in a state of "shuddering with terror." It was then a foregone conclusion that the exposure to death incurred by the project had to be terminated.

Our argument maintained that the two languages—the practical (metaphoric) and the essential (literal–metaphysical)—are antitheticals reconciled only within a carefully pre-arranged structure of ritual communication. The funeral project was taken as a case in point to demonstrate the explosive charge inherent in combining the two. It would also seem that the very subject of death served as a promoter of such a clash between the two languages. In the absence of traditional, well-entrenched teachings and guidance such as religious practices or other established symbolic formulae relating to death, such a clash is indeed likely and potentially powerful. It could be suggested that the relative secularity of members of the U3A and their detachment from church or synagogue attendance was the cause both for initiating the project and aborting it. The project reflected a need for a code of practice to supersede institutionalized arrangements with which members could no longer be fully identified. That gap of uncertainty and confusion generated the attempt to produce a set of practical instructions while at the same time unearthing hidden fears and anxieties. The following statements are taken from respondents' references to the general subject at stake without addressing any specific question. The comments project both the bewilderment at confronting the issue and the necessity to cover it up with some authoritative document:

— "I should like to leave my body for medical use and have so directed in my will, but I must find out if anyone would want it! This would, incidentally, reduce costs. There might be a problem over what to do to mark the passing of someone who is not a member of a religious sect and would not want a memorial service. Simply dumping the corpse on a hospital (which then undertakes disposal) leaves no way of mourning and no sense of finality, which might be psychologically important."

The pressing need to have such confusion dispelled by an agreed set of rules is stated in the following:

— "I should recommend that flowers should be cut down to the minimum and donations sent to a suitable charity. I think it would be of great benefit to all concerned if some questionnaire or form could be devised by medical, clerical professions, to be filled in by anyone making a will, so that all distressing questions such as post-mortem, organ donations, or body donated to medical schools would not need further enquiries or signatures by near relatives."

The will as a document of asserting control over one's posthumous arrangements did not seem to satisfy the following respondent, whose anxieties were of a more religious nature:

— "I have no idea what to do if anyone dies abroad. In France, for instance, the churchyards are all Roman Catholic, and if one was a Protestant, would one be allowed in? If not, where would one be put? I have a disinclination to be buried in a cemetery and would prefer to be put in the earth in an upright position with no coffin, merely a winding sheet. However, this might not be allowed, although I think it is possible if instructions are left in the will and the bishop informed so that the vicar may hallow the plot. If the person was not a Christian, obviously no funeral director would be needed—or would they? I feel it would be a great help if a booklet on the subject could be obtained easily in public libraries or doctor's surgeries, with enough publicity so that most people would know where to get it without having to ask too much. I imagine there are many people who are reticent about the subject and who have to suffer unnecessarily over who to ask and where to go. Maybe there is a booklet but it isn't easily seen—I have never seen one."

A note of despair at the loss of human values in the modern age was voiced by a respondent who also advocated the introduction of alternative arrangements to compensate for the decline:

— "Perhaps there should be a go-between. The doctor and hospital have become too 'remote' and lacking in humanity. Perhaps our whole life/death has already become too technological."

The pursuit of proper instructive documentation to bridge the gulf between the humane and the technological is a reflection of the discrepancy between the two languages, whose realignment requires a "go-between"—a broker straddling the gap between them. The tendency to resort to documentary accounts and to engage in written descriptive practices was a paramount feature of the activities of the research committee. Providing an opportunity to transfix lability and to keep change on hold, the very production of written accounts was itself an object constituting the worldview of members. In that sense, written and ultimately printed and circulated reports produced by members were an important means of reflexivity. They posited a reified manifestation of commenting upon reality, which in turn could be referred to, reflected upon, and treated as a fact in its own right. Chapter 9 deals with that subject of reflexivity by focusing on an attempt by members to recreate their own social imagery through the mirroring devices of a research project that, unlike the previously described aborted studies, came to full fruition.

CHAPTER 9

Space Regained:
The Control of Images

Although knowledge of themselves as elderly people was a declared objective of the research committee, making themselves into objects of study
was considered to be an undesirable consequence of their activities. This
apparent contradiction in terms between the conventionally expected end-
results of a research project and the enhancement of knowledge based on
unreported procedures and findings was due to a number of reasons. The
most important one was widely discussed in the analysis of verbal texts
and reflected the disdain and mistrust expressed by members to conceptual fixations and academic jargon. Another reason was the disturbing
feeling that elderly people are extensively "objectified" by society to the
detriment of their well-being, by their mastery over their own lives being
threatened. A third reason was the reluctance to be identified with any
orthodox form of academia (see chapter 10) and the conviction that the
U3A is primarily a self-help organization whose loyalties lie with its
members rather than with a commitment to the outside world. A fourth
reason was the fear expressed by some members that the full implementation of a research project might not live up to the methodological requirements of rigour and validity, thus exposing the local researcher, as well
as the elderly as a whole, to critical scientific evaluation labelling them
incompetent, ineffectual, and unreliable. This, so it was maintained, can

only support such existing stereotypes of the aged and might further undermine their position in society.

This precarious position in society, as members interpreted it, was the driving force that eventually altered that stance and reversed it to the extent of a fully fledged publication being completed, sold to the public, advertised in the media, reviewed in the national and the professional press, and registered with the Library of Congress. The impetus that led to this change of direction was the realization that the kind of membership composing the U3A enables the organization to put forward the case of and for the elderly in a dignified and respectable manner. Furthermore, it was often suggested that the very existence of the U3A, both in Cambridge and in other places throughout the United Kingdom, might help to transform the place of the aged in society into a more positive and acceptable one. To that end, the U3A engaged itself in extensive advertising, distribution of leaflets, enrolment applications, and newsletters.

This self-documentation, however, did not bear the title of research and hence was regarded as a genuine representation of the organization. In the research committee, the term "research" was seldom used, and when proposals were made to pursue a certain line of inquiry, a great deal of caution and sensitivity was exercised as to its social repercussions and possible usefulness for the aged. Thus, it was suggested that the nutrition of elderly people should be studied, with the intention of compiling a guide giving nutritional advice in order to assist elderly consumers in planning their expenditure and diets. Objection to the idea was raised on the grounds that such an account of the problems of the aged concerning both economy and health might confirm already-existing negative images of the old as poor and sick. Another exhortation was that any such study conducted among Cambridge elderly would endanger their strong position in the community. The decision reached was that such a project could be carried out only on a nation-wide scale. A proposal to take part in a research led by one of Cambridge University's units aiming at gleaning data on the effects of divorce on families was also met with a lack of enthusiasm. The members of the U3A were asked by one of the most prominent members of the organization to interview elderly friends whose parents had divorced. In spite of the revered authority who made that request, members found it difficult to comply. They noted that the association of elderly people with the breakdown of family life might tarnish the only remaining vestige of positive image of the family. The preservation of the cloak of respectability seemed to override other considerations.

This reluctance to mar the social image of the elderly ought to be seen against the backdrop of the high awareness by members of their own faults and follies. Self-mockery was a way to reflect upon such shortcomings as decrepitude, limited life expectancy, and mental degeneration, without risking public opinion. It was even suggested at the research committee, albeit in jest, to have the U3A publish a book of jokes on the aged. This vent for non-perilous reflexivity demonstrates the double-edged dilemma with which members were confronted: striving for more visibility[1] might produce negative social exposure.

Well aware of this trap, members attached a great deal of importance to the control of images and to their own potential to manipulate them. It was taken for granted that the most powerful and all-pervasive shaper of public opinion and cultural myths in our society is television. The impact of the mass media on society was not regarded, however, as a reflection of factual reality or as a propagation of general truths, but, as one of the members put it: "Television caters to what it calls the lowest common denominator, but that common denominator is their own doing, they create the need and then cater to it. In that respect we are no different to Russian television."

The poignant conviction that images are generated by the mass media and, in turn, become true to form culturally endorsed facts made members ponder over the projection of the old on British television. It was argued that if the public could be persuaded that television has a balanced attitude towards the elderly, this might affect the misguided view of the old as pitiful, dependent, and undignified.

This belief in constructing a positive image of the old laid the foundation for the establishment of the research committee whose first enterprise was to probe the feelings of members of the public in the Cambridge marketplace as to the question of whether or not elderly people have the capacity to learn new things. The overwhelming response to this self-denigrating query was affirmative.

All this constituted the background for the most publicized, best-accomplished project carried out by the research committee. It was the systematic monitoring of the image of the elderly on television. A report based on this study was published by the U3A in Cambridge as *Research Report No. 1* (Lambert et al. 1984), as a paperback, printed in a most professional manner under a grant awarded by the Independent Broadcasting Authority. The 12-page booklet containing full details of the procedures, content, and findings of the research received much publicity and was launched at a special press conference held at the Independent Broadcasting Authority's head office in London. Members of the research committee met with journalists and gave a detailed account of their findings and of the methodological procedures employed in obtaining them. This last point seemed to be of particular importance, since it accredited the study with an air of objective credibility that endowed the whole occasion with a spirit of a social academic affair, free from the undesirable undertones of charity. Indeed, a prominent topic of conversation, formal and informal, was the place of the elderly in the community. Television crews, scriptwriters, producers, and directors prided themselves on the full intergenerational integration that their programmes exhibit and project. Coverage of this gathering was given in some newspapers and magazines, and the self-confidence of those members involved was considerably boosted. Other members' encouragement and pride at that achievement strengthened the recognition that the U3A has the power to make society aware of the positive and active role the aged could and should play in it. Moreover, it was regarded as a public affirmation that knowledge of the elderly ought to be mastered and constructed by the elderly themselves. It was a marriage between the U3A as the arbiters of old age and the mass-media representatives as generators of cultural imagery, which empowered the former to assume advocacy of the elderly and exonerated the latter from charges of stereotypization and misrepresentation of the old.

In order to ascertain the components of this congruence between the elderly and the manufacturers of mass-media symbols, it is imperative to decipher the linguistic code inherent in the text of the report. The argument to be pursued is that the encoding of the study, its research design, and its inherent categories wholly subscribed to the metaphoric language of practice, survival, and social images. From the outset, the report shows a great concern to establish its credibility by naming the academic bodies and individuals involved in its making. Such support was given by scholars, by a television research unit at a leading university, and by the research division of the Independent Broadcasting Authority.

Nevertheless, approval by implication of research methods and results did not seem sufficient to guarantee full confidence in the impartiality and competence of the researchers as elderly persons. That objective was instituted by stressing that the 14-member monitoring team who viewed and evaluated television programmes for two weeks included 4 monitors under 60 years of age, the youngest of whom was 33 years old. That fact was presented in conjunction with the lack of a significant difference in the assessment scales of monitors. Another methodological snag was tackled in a similar fashion. The ascription of age to television characters could not be objective, since such information is rarely made available to viewers. The decision, therefore, regarding the inclusion of characters in the assessment had to be subjectively based. The researchers, being aware of this pitfall, which, in their eyes, was not commensurate with the dictates of objectivity in science, used the high degree of uniformity among monitors to offer circumstantial evidence confirming the unbiased nature of their report. The argument of overall consistency in monitors' scales was also applied to the question of the basis of judgement. The "fair"/"unfair" dichotomy as a yardstick for assessing treatment or usage of the elderly is obviously a crude and highly personalized analytic device. Having recognized this, the researchers suggested that the unanimity among members offsets the effect of individual diversity. It is interesting to note that the pursuit of objectivity was revealed in the division of estimated age groups with which monitors had to comply. They were required to place the viewed characters in three predetermined categories: between the ages of 60 and 69; 70 and 79; and 80+. This was expected, despite all reservations, to be done on the basis of, and sometimes in the course of, in the language of the report, "very short periods of time, seconds rather than minutes; such appraisals had to be made very quickly." This was justified by yet another mark of credibility—the monitoring of programmes was done in real time, without the aid of recording or repeat viewing. Credibility of researchees, as well as monitors, was also gained by providing full details of each member's viewing scale, including number of programmes watched and their distribution according to the criterion of fairness. Finally, the report framed itself within the context of the general academic study of the media and the elderly. Quoting an American source, the researchers beg to differ from its findings and to offer their own conclusions. But perhaps the most striking plea for academic recognition and acknowledgement was the authority of Professor P. Laslett, the then chairman of the research committee, whose co-authorship of the report was boldly stated on the cover page and whose foreword introduced the booklet.

All these insignia of credibility were offered to the potential reader of the report to create a common ground for accepting the main result of the study, which is:

> It seems to be almost universally assumed that elderly people are unfavourably treated by television. However true of other countries, from which hostile stereotypes are so often reported, especially from the United States where much of the research has been done, this cannot be said to be true of Britain.

It elaborates this by saying that both BBC and ITV project generally "fair" and "just" images of the elderly, even though "the elderly appear on British television far less often than is justified by their proportion in the population and their importance in people's experience." This comment attests to the assumption that television is expected by the researchers to be a faithful mirror of reality, and in that sense its monitoring could provide a true image of society's attitude towards the old. As the report concludes:

> There is evidence, however, that in thinking of old people in real life, the public in general affirm the positive attitudes of the elderly and reject the negative.

This anticipated compatibility between the media and society renders the study exceedingly important, since its findings ought to be regarded as a reflection of the standing of the elderly in society at large. Such congruence was inherent in the research design and execution, which were both based on the components of the metaphoric language of practice—in other words, accepting the edifice of the prevailing social structure as well as the main social assumptions viewing the elderly in terms of adjustment and maladjustment to that structure. The language of adaptation, survival, and conformity determined the course and the results of the study, which, in turn, served that very same purpose of promoting means of better fit between the old and their social environment. A testimony to this argument was given in the use the report made of two semantic zones of that language, the first being the British class system and the second the array of properties of adaptability. Both terminologies were rigidly separated from the metonymic language of the textual discourse. It would seem that narrowing the gap between the elderly and society required the abandonment of the latter in favour of the former.

The finding regarding the positive treatment of the elderly on television was supported by the observation that most portrayals of elderly persons on factual programmes were of rich male characters. This was based on the following breakdown of the class-system:

• higher managerial/professional

• managerial/professional

• clerical etc.

• manual skilled

• manual unskilled

• unemployed

Evidently, this division does not parallel the distinction between "upper" and "lower," "ruling" versus "working," etc. Occupationally based, this structure avoids insinuations of being upper-class-slanted without abandoning the fundamental notion of class itself. Analytically, no differentiation was offered between "status" and "class," and the two were accorded an identical meaning:

In 222 programmes it was possible to assess the social status of elderly individuals. Rather more than 51% were from the Higher Professional/ Managerial classes, including politicians and political leaders who represented 40% of the group.

These data, although refuting the claim of negative images of the elderly on television, bothered the researchers a great deal, since they indicated an incongruity between images and reality:

> These figures show that the representation of the class composition of the
> elderly on television is as severely distorted as the representation of their
> sex composition. Over four fifths of all those appearing seem to belong to
> the managerial and professional class, upper and lower, which is surpris-
> ing even taking account of the fact that viewers may be more interested in
> the wealthy and the powerful than in people like themselves.

Seeking consistency between social structure and the place of the aged
in it was a claim for inclusion and acceptability. The other semantic zone
of terms of reference to the old reflected the two poles of that acceptability—properties of adjustment versus markers of maladjustment. In a section of the report entitled "Characterization of the Elderly by British
Television," a list of 15 pairs of contrasting attributes of elderly people
was applied as tests for the various images projected on television. Each
pair of opposites was employed to measure the proportion of negative
versus positive appearances of elderly characters representing corresponding images. The response to each pair was subdivided into three estimated
age-groups (60–69; 70–79; 80+). The significance of this list is not so
much in its composition (see below) but in its being a product of self-
knowledge and personal images of the elderly research rather than a testimony to any scientifically endorsed chart. This self-presentation was a
language underpinned by a fit or otherwise between the old and society. It
included the following dichotomies:

1. wise/foolish
2. active/passive
3. fit/infirm
4. content/discontent
5. dignified/undignified
6. pleasant/unpleasant
7. comfortable/badly off
8. tolerant/intolerant
9. neat/ untidy
10. authoritative/powerless
11. competent/incompetent
12. effective/ineffective

13. respected/not respected

14. independent/dependent

15. sexually active/inactive

All the "positive" sides tipped the balance to various extents in all age groups and in all 15 categories. What is striking, however, about this vocabulary is that it mixes together factually ascertainable variables and competence with highly subjective determinants such as appearance, tolerance and wisdom. This in itself is no different from monitor-based questionnaires. The difference, however, lies with the authority, by virtue of being old themselves, exercised by the researchers to enlist those images as a composite portrait of old age. The authorship of that portrayal, namely the right and authority to depict, which was mastered by the old, enabled them to transcend the personal into the social, the subjectively forbidden into the objectively endorsed. The mixed vocabulary was a double-edged device, translating old age from experienced knowledge into shared knowledge at the expense of complying with stereotypes of adaptability. This kind of authority was asserted in a number of unequivocal observations made by monitors to describe, in terms of this mixed vocabulary, some of their viewing impressions: "In children's programmes the elderly were often presented in cartoons as white-haired, bespectacled, eccentric 'dears,' ladies with 'buns' . . ." or "In comedy programmes . . . the distressing traits of old age were made fun of: incontinence, handicaps of sight and hearing, making the elderly undignified and unworthy of respect . . ." or ". . . passive, infirm and inactive elderly . . ." or ". . . foolish, infirm, incompetent, not respected and ineffective."

The potency of this social language was a means for reclaiming a position in society, albeit of limited liability. The dilemma of circumventing the traps of the two languages to create a context where the essential could be accommodated alongside the practical was the pivot around which the construction of the setting of the U3A revolved.

CHAPTER **10**

Reason Applied:
The Void of Autonomy

Negotiating for a "third age" did not stop with the inception of the U3A. To remain loyal to its cause, this organization had to secure maximum freedom of selecting content and substance within rigid boundaries protecting against the patronizing intervention of the non-aged from the outside and the ominous threats of deterioration and death coming from within.

An appropriate vantage-point from which to start the discussion of this self-sufficient context would be by referring to chapter 9 and the case of the report on television and the image of the elderly. Showered with congratulatory gestures, from the media as well as from other members, the researchers were encouraged and, indeed, keen to disseminate the report in the circles of the U3A. A token charge for members was fixed, and the opportunity to purchase the booklet was widely publicized. The sale rate, however, was well below expectations, and a great number of copies remained unsold. Neither disapproval nor lack of interest, and certainly not financial considerations, can explain this avoidance (for such an approach see Hazan 1986). The response was rendered even more ambivalent in the light of members' enthusiastic willingness to participate in a host of rather costly functions, including theatre shows, dinners, trips abroad, and procuring expensive working material for their courses. Consistent with the model of the interstice between the two languages that leaves room for endless manoeuvres with the minimum of commitment, that attitude could be understood as a reluctance by members to institute themselves as objects of knowledge. It was already suggested that members were disinclined to offer themselves as objects for any kind of purpose (see previous chapter). Being an object, even of self-knowledge, might considerably curtail the freedom members enjoyed to exercise choice without the restraints of antecedents and consequences. What seems at first a contradiction in terms—an organizational framework without a system of cultural artifacts[1]—was established at the U3A by virtue of its set-up, which was based on the pursuit of practical solutions unaccompanied by a corresponding symbolic order of moral codes, prestige insignia, and prescribed modes of behaviour.

The ambivalent relationship with the "sister university," as members used to call it—namely, the University of Cambridge—could be taken as an example for the dilemma of being an organization without distinct symbolic content. Proud as they were to be part of the Cambridge intellectual ambience, the liaison with "the other University"—yet another term to describe that link in a somewhat cynical spirit—was regarded as being problematic. The patron of the U3A at the time of the research was Sir John Butterfield, O.B.E., Master of Downing College and Vice Chancellor of Cambridge University, and the Chairman was Professor Peter Laslett, a fellow of Trinity College. With such strong sponsorship, it could have been expected that the U3A would foster that relationship, to become more closely affiliated with that prestigious academic establishment. Members, however, rejected offers made by Cambridge University to strengthen ties and let the U3A operate under its auspices. This position was taken despite some obvious advantages that could have been gained from such an arrangement, particularly with regard to the pressing accommodation problems the U3A suffered due to its rapid growth. Resisting such temptations was accounted for by uncompromising insistence on autonomy. That autonomy was described by members in terms of being a self-help organization assuming full and sole responsibility for the course of studies. The self-presentation of the U3A organization was strictly confined to administrative and financial matters, with the space allocated for the curriculum being completely free of any influences. In fact, the diffuse nature of the spectrum of courses offered to and by members was so varied and non-committal to the idea of educational academic pursuit that some members proposed that the word "university" should be omitted from the title (see chapter 4), and instead the very diverse character of activities should be addressed. This is an additional explanation for the unwillingness to form a closer association with the University of Cambridge.

The autonomous status of the U3A was sustained by a rapidly growing membership "without special promotion and mostly by word of mouth recommendation," as one of the newsletters phrased it. Incepted on the Easter of 1982, the U3A in Cambridge had 500 members at the time of the research. The division between male and female members was equal, and not 66% females and 33% males, as in the total population. The reason given by members was that, unlike men, who are lonely after their retirement and need the company, most women are still engaged in former social networks. The overall majority of the members were middle-class and upwards. There was no "working class" in the U3A of Cambridge, mainly because its hard core of founders belonged to the University of Cambridge, and this elitist nucleus attracted its own kind. It should be noted that even this very basic set of data was hard to come by, since members refused to relate to themselves in such terms. Furthermore, it was the policy of the management of the U3A not to query participants as to level of income, educational background, past careers, and social standing. The registration form (see below) distributed for the purpose of enrolment to courses sought scant information, confined only to the required courses and the type of registration fee—annual or life membership. This last option spells a token of fully fledged commitment to the organization as well as a suggestion of immutable identification with the "third age" rather than the "fourth."

Members selected at their annual meeting a Management Committee consisting of 12 yearly appointed representatives, which included the chairperson and the treasurer. Accountable to that committee was a three-member management team comprising the director of studies, the administrator, and a financial officer. The organization is voluntary-based; courses are proposed and lectured by local members, with a few exceptions, such as employing a two-member paid clerical team and hiring some language teachers. The rest of the operation conforms to the idea of self-help and mutual teaching. The financial outlay for running the organization comes from annual membership fees (£20 in 1984), course fees, donations, some public funds, and individual bequests made by members.

This formal structure did not develop into a hierarchical, bureaucratic body concerned mainly with the accumulation and preservation of power. Various reasons account for that phenomenon. Unlike other charities, which serve a target clientele, the U3A appeals to a vast yet unknown population, in which "with no membership barriers of age, experience or education, interests are pursued for themselves alone rather than for the achievement of qualification," as stated in a U3A flier. With such broad definitions of potential membership the organization does not cater for any specific need and offers no career opportunities. Under such circumstances the contractual relationship between the organization and its members is extremely tenuous and entails no firm commitment or undertaking on either side. This is a non-cumulative transaction, which is difficult to transform into human capital producing expendable resources. The rigid boundaries set between the U3A and its organizational milieu hamper any attempt to trade off its output for any conceivable returns. The only exception to that self-imposed isolation was the association that evolved between the Cambridge U3A and other U3A's around the country, though even these connections could have been construed as a threat to self-sufficiency, and the U3A newsletter found it necessary to allay such fears by reassuring its readers that: "Although the U3A in Cambridge is completely autonomous, it is associated with a wide variety of similar organizations throughout the country, and there is a National Committee which meets from time to time to consider ways of fostering the development of these activities." These loose ties with non-competing peers sharing the same convictions was an asset rather than a risk and, in fact, promoted autonomy by legitimizing its ideological foundation and reaffirming its localized emphasis.

Organizational structure alone cannot account for the egalitarian nature of the U3A. The human factor involved in the running and daily operation of the organization is of prime importance to the understanding of the absence of emergent bureaucratic properties. First, the age of members, as well as their considerable geographical mobility, caused a relatively high turnover of both rank-and-file members and incumbents of official positions. The membership life-expectancy of a newcomer to the organization was fairly short, due to deterioration in mental and physical state. The unspoken subject of hospitalization, institutionalization, and being taken care of by family was a cause for members' disappearance from the scene of the U3A. Conversely, members who, due to their state of retirement, were free to move around and had no financial worries, took advantage of this last opportunity to live in other places and even experience emigration. This combination of change in health, conditions, and the freedom to choose a suitable life-style brought about constant fluctuations in the size of membership as well as in the individuals comprising it.

The determinants of fluidity, coupled with a conviction of fundamental equality prevailing among members (see chapter 6), made for a rather informal atmosphere in all official meetings of the organization. Members were not intimidated by status and title, and they aired their views, critical and sarcastic as they sometimes were, in an open and straightforward manner. Heckling, jeering, and cross-talk were commonplace at meetings, and loosely programmed agenda helped the emergence of a free-for-all arena of exchanging opinions, putting forward suggestions, and making personal comments—"Aren't we a lively lot?" was one remark out of many made at a general meeting that represented the effervescent mood dominating such gatherings. This style of interaction gave vent to the proliferation of a whole web of informal contacts and unmonitored behaviour, which embraced activities at all levels and produced a host of unofficial encounters concerned with the running and character of the organization. The very nature of the daily activities, which included social functions such as luncheons and outings, facilitated and reinforced that trend.

This kind of free market of ideas and activities became so widespread that it might have undermined the already loosely constructed edifices of the organization and rendered it superfluous. Having realized that even this minimum of control over the flow of operation was getting out of hand, the management team set up a "communication group" to furnish it with current knowledge of what was going on among members. Or, as it was put to members in a newsletter in the "administrative" announcement of the creation of this group:

> In a voluntary organization such as U3A it is always difficult to ensure that relevant information reaches everyone and for the right hand to know what the left hand is doing.

This rationale provided the basis for the mandate within which the committee was expected to carry out its assigned function. These included two areas of regulating the flow of information—inside the U3A and outside it. In our terms, it was thought to be in charge of sustaining the internal void while maintaining its boundaries. In the phrasing of the committee's charter, it was stated that it would "oversee the various information sheets issued to members (including the newsletter)," and "act as a clearing house for suggestions and new initiatives coming from within U3A Cambridge and again refer them for any necessary action." The contacts with the outside were to be safeguarded, as the committee was responsible to "check our publicity material and liaise as necessary with local press and radio" and to sift through "field enquiries from outside bodies (including other U3A's) and refer them for action if necessary."

Having established its parameters of accountability, the committee had to persuade members to cooperate in the implementation of a policy that might not have been consistent with their conception of their own involvement in the U3A. The following plea for collaboration made by the chairwoman of the committee reveals the dilemma of introducing a sense of order into an inherently labile and unstructured situation. Presented as a "proposal" rather than a request or a demand, the statement argues its case:

> In a self-generating organization such as ours there is always room for new enterprise and energy to carry things forward. If you are as yet not actively engaged, and feel that you might be able to deputize for someone who is already undertaking work of some kind, or if you have a new proposition to put forward, you may like to know that we are hoping to have an open meeting in the New Year at which people already involved might meet those who are prepared to help and perhaps double-bunk them if it should be necessary.

Explicit in this call is the attempt to equalize involvement among members, thereby lessening concentration of loci of impact in the hands of a few members. Implicit in it is the realization that controlling the "energy" of members cannot be contained within a superimposed framework.

The most striking evidence for that assumption is the framework set by the organization itself to accommodate the various activities it promotes.[2] Before scanning the programme of studies offered by the U3A, it should be pointed out that the claim for minimal qualifications made by the organization is well reflected in the registration form, which seeks the most basic information about applicants. Name and address are the only items asked for to be eligible to pay the required fee and enrol. Admission to certain courses, particularly at an advanced level of languages, is, however, conditional upon the candidate meeting some academic prerequisites. This minimum of primary requirements deliberately stems from the issue of equality.

The list of courses offered, although sectioned into eight divisions, is subsumed under one programme of studies ranging from classical languages to sport. Alongside "conventional" courses given on the premises, there were also special seminars held in the homes of housebound tutors. The first one to start this series was a study group looking at the history of apartheid in South Africa. The tutor was a lady, Mrs. Franklin, who had lived for many years in that country and, on returning to England and settling in Cambridge, became an enthusiastic member of the Cambridge U3A (see also Futerman 1984:131). Characteristic of the diffuse nature of activities in the U3A was an exhibition put on by the fine arts classes and staged at the central library, where brush-painted or written Chinese poems (drawn by the Chinese study group) as well as poems produced by the "writers' cycle," a small showcase containing diet study sheets and recipe books (made by the nutrition seminar) and a collage of photos from the trip to Hadrian's Wall (undertaken by the history group) were all exhibited too (Futerman, 1984).

The seemingly obvious observation that members are exposed to an undifferentiated pool of choices is, however, somewhat altered by the order of divisions appearing in the list of courses, which does spell an implicit hierarchy of importance, with languages at the top and recreation at the bottom:

1. Languages (including French, German, Greek—classical and modern— Italian, Latin, Russian, Spanish, and Swedish).

2. Literature (mainly English, but also Czech, namely Milaan Kundera).

3. History (including history of the English language and English Literature, history of the English countryside, and history of Cambridge).

4. General (see below).

5. Music (including theory and practice—playing and singing).

6. Art (including art history, heraldry, and painting classes).

7. Gardening and the countryside (including country houses, ecology, and bird-watching).

8. Recreation (chess, bridge, pewter, sport, and many more pastimes).

A review of the subjects would show a distinct classification of courses into basic areas of knowledge such as classical languages, literature, and history on the one hand and applied pursuits, such as embroidery, fitness exercises, and modern languages—which, incidentally, were in great de-mand—on the other. This dichotomy is rendered even sharper if we con-sider the fact that no course concerning the sciences was offered (except for a *New Scientist* reading group). This impression is accentuated in view of the considerable number of medically and scientifically qualified mem-bers. The lesson that could be drawn from this apparent contradiction is significant to the clarification of the distinction between the two lan-guages.

It would seem that what is considered to fall into the category of the "essential" amounts to spheres of already established and partly acquired knowledge, which members wished to expand and deepen. Those were domains of what was conceived of as vitally embedded constituents in one's intellectual infrastructure, of which no practical use can be made and, indeed, should not be expected. Conversely, applied knowledge is readily available and instantly implementable. It could be put to some valuable practice to help improve personally desirable skills, competence, aptitude, and physical state. In that respect, embroidery, chess, bridge, Chinese exercises, gardening, and knowledge of country homes are indi-vidual pastimes and pursuits that could be advanced by participation in relevant classes.

Nevertheless, this distinction does not necessarily correspond to the breakdown of courses reflected in the eight divisions cited. A closer ex-amination of the content of courses and particularly of the ways by which that content was conveyed to members reveals that most classes were presented by their tutors or leaders as possible arenas for free discourse where competing ideas and open discussions could emerge and evolve. Only very few courses offered frontal teaching methods, and these were mainly in the discipline of language, where systematic training was required. A number of quotations from the syllabus describing the expected form of classroom interaction might demonstrate this preferred mode of learning:

French advanced conversation:
Concentrates on modern French, play and novel reading, tapes, radio programmes, discussion of current issues, etc.

Poetry:
Members of the group will decide which opinion they prefer, since participation will form an integral part of the meetings.

Theology:
The emphasis is on discussion aimed at increasing understanding. Questions guaranteed—answers less likely.

This last course was included under the heading of the "General" division and, like most of the other classes offered within that vague category, it represents an acutely attuned scene for potential discourse free of the constrictions of a specific subject-matter. This kind of arena was introduced into the programme of studies in the wake of increasing requests by members to have such frameworks for open debate on current affairs, general problems, and relevant issues to members in the official syllabus of the U3A. Such courses lent themselves to becoming stages of unadulterated discourse where members could act out the interplay between the principles of the two languages. Some brief pre-course descriptions of the anticipated nature of these classes could demonstrate their plausibility to serve such functions.

Image and Meaning:
This is not a consecutive course, but, rather, a study group and shared cumulative inquiry whereby we attempt to understand the meanings manifest or implicit in works of art. . . . Often members of the group volunteer to give talks on subjects they have studied.

Philosophical Revisions:
. . . how did the universe originate and what sort of a universe is it. Puzzles about our way of thinking—problems of logic, language and perception. How do I know that I know? And why should I be good? Ethics, morals and politics. Religious problems in a sceptical world. Existence and nature of God. Body, soul and mind related psychological problems.

The third age preoccupied two courses whose approach was mainly practical:

Living in the Third Age:
An exploration of the problems and challenges of life in the 3rd age and discussion of coping mechanisms. Preference will be given to new members. [This last caveat presents the course as a step of initiation into the enclave of the U3A.]

Psychology:
. . . this course will be slanted in particular towards people of the "third age" and it is hoped that those attending will contribute a great deal from their own experiences.

Sharing experience and knowledge was also the main motif of the last course in this division, entitled "The Eclectics," where "members will in turn introduce and chair a discussion or read a paper on a subject of mutual interest."

This brings the discussion back to the possibility of the text analysed in the second part of this book and to the impossibility of the discourse of learning outlined in the first part. Texts composed of the dialectic between the two languages were the products of exchanges within the void created by the setting of the U3A. Those exchanges, however, were not acts of learning. Rather, they were exploration and experimentation of a new reason separating essence from practice. It is only now that we are in a position to appreciate this observation fully. In order to reach such understanding, however, we had to proceed through the invisible maze of the elderly voices and their verbal texts. It is now, I think, that the reason behind the inverted logic of this book—from discourse, to text, to context, rather than the other way around—becomes clear. For the context of the U3A, in which we now stand, lies in fact in its discourse; whereas the anthropological discourse ensnaring it should be seen as its context of presentation.

It is appropriate to conclude this chapter by referring to an intriguing characteristic of the activities of the U3A. Among the great variety of recreational pastimes offered to members, the dramatic sphere of playing and acting was conspicuous in its absence. There could be a host of possible interpretations to these lacunae. Nevertheless, consistently with the arguments propounded in our discussion, it could be suggested that the gulf between the two languages does not allow for the pursuit of culturally dependent meaning in the form of enactment of assumed roles or theatrical disguise.[3] The control over meaning, illusory as it is, instilled in dramatic performance defied the fundamental principle of keeping the two worlds—of true meaning and false appearance—apart.

CHAPTER 11

Discussion:
An Experiment in Ageing

The absence of contrived dramatic performance among the varied activities promoted by the U3A may attest to a more general feature of its members' behaviour—the refraining from role-taking. Members did not present themselves as playing roles of leadership, class advocates, ex-military, community stalwarts, local politicians, or teachers. They did not dwell on past occupations and statuses as trappings of their present situation, nor did they switch from one identity to another. The wearing and shedding of masks did not figure in their overall demeanour, and concepts so often used with regard to the elderly (sometimes with an assumed therapeutic merit), such as "acting out," "enacting," and "re-enacting" (particularly life histories),[1] could not be cogently applied to this arena.

Notwithstanding the validity of such claims and their socio-psychological significance,[2] the lack of the dramatic element among members could serve as a useful vantage-point from which to embark on this concluding discussion. At first sight, it seems to find obvious support in my former argument: since role-playing distracts the person further from his "essence" and statuses discard equality, the former must be eradicated so that the latter might re-emerge. Furthermore, it may suggest that the elderly in question did not develop any meta-linguistic formation capable of transferring one experiential sphere to another, thereby translating one type of linguistic expression to the rules and content of another. Play and rituals, being devices capable of such transformations and hence possessing meta-communicative properties, were not a variety of the range of social forms pursued by members. The crux of the ensuing argument is devoted to the intricacies of this omission and to its concomitant issue of the modes of articulation chosen by members.

There are many possible ways of construing the material at hand, and each within the bounds of its basic assumptions may be as valid as any other. Ageing, however defied and denied by members, is—perhaps due to this—our general framework to set the explanatory scene for understanding the data.

Two crucial boundaries confined members to the self-imposed sanctuary of the U3A. The one, which they had already crossed, was that of retirement; the other, looming ominously before them, was that of possible deterioration, decrepitude, disability, social denigration, and ultimately death. Charged with the wisdom of the former, namely their past, and furnished by the opportunities of the present, members were, consciously or otherwise, preparing themselves for the future. The enterprise of the U3A is, hence, as I argued from the preface onward, an experiment in ageing.

I chose to use the term "experiment" for a number of reasons. The U3A setting was relatively secluded from other areas of life, and the open license it provided for free-floating ideas and for the introduction of novel, sometimes non-conformist conceptions set it as a living laboratory. The scientifically minded attitude of the members, who endeavoured to make sense of the world by the application of logical and rational procedures, made that laboratory into a controlled arena of negotiating ideas and implementing corresponding patterns of behaviour. That controllability meant that everyday life did not have to be immediately affected by the results of the experiments conducted, though lessons could be learnt and conclusions drawn to be saved for an hour of need. Finally, the strong intellectual drive that motivated members to enquire into their own existence, without necessarily applying the findings of that study to their lives, endowed the whole set-up with an air of an academic exercise. The title of the organization, coupled with the powerful, imposing surroundings of Cambridge, also contributed to the making of a setting fit for scientific work.

The notion of experiment entails some pre-meditated consequence, some end to be revealed by its means. Throughout this book, I have ventured to demonstrate how members of the U3A were continuously engaged in a distinct pattern of behaviour, revolving around the object of literacy (but not learning) and carried through numerous discussions, which presented a unique kind of discourse striving for first principles and conducted under accepted rules. Some of these rules we defined as "basic," and certain discussions were, respectively, regarded as "accountable" or not. It is in this final part of the analysis that the ways of researchees and researcher are bound to part, since the latter attributes some sense of motivation and purpose, and thereby inevitably of meaning, to the former. In this respect, then, the argument boils down to the question of purpose. In simpler terms: did members know what they were engaged in, or didn't they?

It is my conviction that they knew the means as well as the ends of that practice. How one interprets the meaning of "knowledge" is evidently a complex question in itself. Is it something general, basic, deeper than appearances, or is it solely performative practice, application? To use Wittgenstein's (1953) example, does someone who knows how to count to 100 know the set of natural numbers? It seems that this philosophical riddle would be accounted for as a case in point by members too; moreover, it becomes apparent that we are now engaged in their own discourse, the discourse of the two opposite modes of articulation.

I argue that the "purpose" of this discourse must be sought in the existential conditions of its participants. Its acceptance by all U3A members attests, I think, to its adaptive value. The ends of participation in the U3A hence determined the means of participation. This logical nexus between means and ends is significant because their separation has notably been postulated to be a prime criterion of play and fantasy (Miller 1973; Handelman 1990). The fact that such separation does not occur is therefore consistent with my previous observation of the omission of dramatic elements from the U3A world. While separation of means from ends is a pre-requisite of play, its cohesion is the logical tenet of the experiment.

This impression cannot be complete without considering some other conspicuously missing elements in the behaviour of members, whose presence could have negated the notion of the experimental form. Members, as amply indicated before, did not indulge in reminiscing; nor did they dwell on past histories. They were not caught up in streams of timeless consciousness, nor did they dedicate their meetings to the quest for meaning. Their mental alacrity and their intellectual faculties were geared to processes of inference based on fact-finding rather than heart-searching and to ways of sequential deduction rather than lateral thinking. This is not to say that such alternative modes of reasoning were not to be found—perhaps they prevail in other areas of their lives. It merely suggests that the kind of atmosphere and the character of the setting dominating the U3A allow us to confer the concept of experimentation upon the activities, particularly those concerning the production of verbal texts as presented in this book.

PARADOXES OF PRODUCING AND CONSUMING
KNOWLEDGE IN THE U3A

Old people are usually conceived of as passive consumers of knowledge, even that which precipitates their exclusion from the rest of society
such as the domains of medicine, welfare, and employment. There is an
inverse relation between the consumption of those cultural products and
their implication for the old. The more such knowledge is needed, the less
socially acceptable the consumer is, and the greater the power exerted
upon her or him to be excluded from social life. Elderly people know that
by frequenting the doctor's surgery, by claiming welfare benefits, by going to O.A.P. (old-age pensioner) clubs and by using facilities designed
for the old, they designate themselves as social outcasts. Knowledge is
indeed power, as many sociologists would have it, but in the case of the
elderly, this nexus is to the detriment of its consumer. Members of the
U3A, however, created a setting for generating knowledge about themselves which does not entail an adverse effect on their lives and which
could even be traded to the world of the non-aged as legitimate, useful,
and enlightening—see, for example, the case of the report on the image of
the elderly on British television.

Furthermore, that knowledge which was self-produced was also, in the
main, self-consumed. The question of the properties of that self-knowledge are of prime importance, not only to the understanding of its value to
its immediate consumers, but to the assessment of its applicability to the
non-aged. In other words, if the discrepancy between conventional socio-
anthropological conceptual modes and that self-knowledge of ageing is
unbridgeable, then the former is unlikely to benefit from the latter or even
to give it the credit it deserves as an intellectual endeavour worthy of
academic and possibly social attention.

We shall start this inquiry into the nature of that knowledge by positing
an apparent paradox. Recent trends in the sociology of ageing—some
appearing under the vaguely defined stream of "postmodernism"—maintain that the life course and its ascribed stages are socially manufactured,[3]
thus restricting real knowledge of ageing and genuine, ageless expression
of authenticity by the aged (see Featherstone & Hepworth 1990). Fluency
of personal continuity is thus regarded as a prerequisite for breaking down
the social barriers of cultural stereotypes impeding access to the masked
world of the elderly (Featherstone & Hepworth 1991). The elderly in our
case do not attest to this proposition. Conversely, by cocooning themselves in the social capsule of the third age, they freed their minds and
actions from a whole load of social impositions that would have impinged
upon their outlook and prospects. This view of the emancipated state of
the elderly within and perhaps due to the confines of their age group is

also shared by some scholars (e.g. Moody 1988), who appreciate the potential held in store for and by the elderly in such protectorates, be they socially constructed or self-imposed or, as is usually the case—both. Such a state of liberation from stunting social constraints might release in the elderly a capacity to provide a type of self-knowledge, based neither on conforming to social texts of "rolelessness" and powerlessness nor on structured expectations to produce evidence of their "inner selves" and their life narratives.[4] Rather, they are potentially able to generate "writerly" texts,[5] free of conventions irrelevant to their being in the world and open to endless rewriting and reformulation. The verbal rendition, as well as the written description produced by members, could be described as such open-ended texts, since they were, as we have studied, free of—or at least critical of—social formulae and cultural codes. These are texts of what could be termed "local knowledge"[6] which reflect, by virtue of their context, the descriptive activity pertaining[7] to knowledge of ageing.

Here another paradox is embedded. These texts reach a high degree of openness mainly due to the fact that their authors declined to see themselves as objects of their own knowledge—that is, as old. Hence, their reluctance to present themselves to themselves as "others" (see the discussion of "othering" in chapter 2) aborts the possibility of the non-aged, or any outsider for that matter, treating them as "others"; thus, they remain subjects[8] rather than objects.

By being engaged in this kind of problematic situation of relating to themselves as objects, members accorded themselves a position of vicarious anthropologists, whose grappling with the complexity of "othering" their subjects and themselves is well documented in their writings.[9] If this analogy is rendered acceptable, then the members' experiment in ageing could also be studied as an anthropological discourse in its own right. As such, it should be treated as a twofold experiment, pertinent to the understanding of ageing as much as to the addressing of anthropological concerns through the eyes of the elderly researchers. The "professional" anthropologist, however, finds it hard to resist the temptation of drawing on that experiment to learn about the limits of gerontological anthropology to study ageing and, indeed, about the horizons of anthropology as a whole. If the two experimental strands are to be recapitulated in an interrogative form, two parallel questions could be posed: What kind of anthropological knowledge was produced by members? And what kind of anthropological understanding can be gained from it?

What is required to tackle these questions amounts to deciphering the members' method of anthropological inquiry and their way of constructing knowledge on their own ground, but in anthropologically acceptable terms.

Notwithstanding the imperative of a shared code for communicating members' outlook to the anthropological community, it would seem that some fundamental obstacles ought to be overcome before such a translation is rendered intelligible. If the gap between subject and object disappeared in members' thinking, then the source of constructing a lingo by extrapolating observed reality into conceptual reifications is missing. Moreover, as members were preoccupied with procedures of dismantling and undoing the underpinnings of observed reality, together with its conceptual filtering devices and intellectual templates, their work could be seen as a form of counter-conceptualization, or a deconstruction of the architecture of the world they had known. Further complication is incurred by the fact that not only was previous knowledge and the taken-for-granted the objective of this process of dissection, but the very basic tools with which it was performed (e.g. language, history, evolution, cultural context and structure) could also not withstand its scrutiny and were, themselves, questioned and largely discredited. How are we to learn about unlearning, to understand procedures that defy the breeding grounds of the conceptual foundation of anthropological scholarship? The puzzlement is even greater in view of the fact that members represent to anthropology an almost ideal subject who is neither self-alienated nor of unknown culture. Not excused by the concessions of old age and not accused of management of impression for the sake of society, members' deconstruction of the world challenges our own ability, not only to understand the world, but even to develop a discourse concerning this understanding. The inevitable fact for some that old age is bound to be entered sooner or later in their life course makes the urge to pave a credible road of gaining access to this world even more pressing.

It would have been relatively comfortable to walk in the footsteps of many others, who view old age either as an exercise in survival and adaptation or, alternatively, as an existential attempt for achieving personal redemption and meaningfulness.[10] The trouble is that neither option was taken by members, who did not take stock of their lives and did not use the U3A to satisfy daily material needs. With the abandonment of identity-oriented explanations and the irrelevance of a problem-solving approach, the nature and purpose of members' activities become even more enigmatic.

Even though the perspective primarily adopted in this discussion is of viewing those activities as an intellectual endeavour towards a new and different understanding of the world, the functional aspect of the purpose served by such an enterprise must not be overlooked, since it was probably of supreme importance to the people in question. It is therefore argued that the procedures and the questions underlying the experiment might have far-reaching repercussions on members' future life. It is further maintained that by using their analytic faculties, members generated, within the social vacuum of the setting, an examination of optional space of alternatives and possibilities of managing old age. In that sense, what we called "an experiment" was, indeed, an experiment in ageing, not only at the level of understanding and consciousness, but also at the level of practical plausibilities.

Broadly speaking, the research question with which members had to deal was the possibility, prospect, and implication of getting out of Plato's cave. What they grappled with in their verbal texts was the separation between the essential and its images, or between the world of forms and that of representations. What they were looking for was nothing short of an "ideal language"—that language sought after, perhaps not by pure coincidence, in the very university of Cambridge early in our century by Russell, Whitehead, and other Cambridge logicians, including the "early" Wittgenstein—a language that, according to a later articulation by Gellner (1973:154), "observes the rule of 'one thing, one name'"—a language in which sense and reference are inextricably identical, and reality corresponds to its representation—a language that is no deceiver, does not mislead, and where impermissible inferences are evident in the very notation. The quest for the essential through procedures of deconstruction was hence an attempt to transfix a category of pure and primordial ideas, whose timeless immutability stands in contrast to its opposite—the domain of passing images and transient phenomena. The perfect form of the being-in-itself and the shadowy representation that masks it—the distinction between these was a key, differentiating between two kinds of lives: the real and the apparent, the perennial and the ephemeral. Having discovered this, members were able to proceed by erecting insurmountable walls between the two, so that appearances and impressions are not mistaken for the real thing. It is hard to overestimate the potential personal benefits of such a separation in the world of ageing, where the demands of social constraints could easily be construed as a fair reflection of the aged. The capacity to live in two different domains—that of the essential, which is taken to be real, and that of the practical, which is taken to be false—is a survival mechanism that, without resorting to meaning and subjective search for it, enables people to endure the ravages of the latter without submitting the former to its own devastating effects. Evidently, members were not subjected to that dilemma in their everyday lives, but the imminence of ageing, of which they were only too aware, was looming heavily over them. Installing a series of undying reference points of certainty in a state where uncertainty, change, and dying are to be the main determinants is a way of securing a modicum of immortality on the margins of mortality.[11]

While preparing for the future, members indulged themselves in an intellectual exercise that assumed knowledge to be bred by idealism, and false knowledge to be originated by images of mass media and representations. The philosophical and anthropological equivalents[12] of this debate between idealistic formations and phenomenological practices (see Ortner 1984) are obvious and not necessarily concealed from members. It must be remembered that many members' past academic training was based on the classics, and Plato's philosophical legacy was not alien to most of them. It is hard to establish, however, to what extent that background impinged upon their present outlook. Since the only available database lending itself to our examination is the collection of verbal and written texts, the question of their origins has to remain a moot one. Plato, of course, is not the only comparable source of ideas. In line with their "writerly" character, other writers can be read between the lines of the texts, such as, for instance, Goethe, whose philosophy of nature conceived of all the plant's parts as successive permutations of a basic organ, which he calls "leaf." Here, he says, the true Proteus lies hidden. This notion of *Dauer im Wechsel* [continuity within change], so similar to the conception the elderly have of the common denominator of humanness evolving within repetitive cycles of events, finds poetic articulation in Goethe's remarkable *Metamorphose der Pflanzen* [Metamorphosis of Plants]:

Always changing, firm persisting,
Near and far and far and near,
Thus in forming and transforming —
To your wonder I am here.

It is intriguing to recall Goethe's words that "in his mind's eye" he beholds the idea of "the original identity of all the vegetal parts" (quoted in Vietor 1950:32). Beholding the original identity of things, then, can be achieved only with a special kind of eyesight—either that of the mind's eye or that of the third-age eye.

THE THREE LANGUAGES RECONSIDERED

At this point of the discussion, it would seem appropriate to return to the opening discourse of the book and reappraise the proposition regarding the mode of articulation predominating in the narrative renditions reproduced in the texts. The three possibilities of expression suggested at the first part of the book—the literal (and old age), metaphoric (middle age) and metaphysical (old age)—were all used by U3A members. However, this usage was directed towards the separation of these three languages, which members viewed as representing different and mutually exclusive modes of reckoning. The stripping from discourse its cultural and contextual vestiges to uncover its essentials was one of the most arduous endeavours attempted by members. The narrative sign that accompanied that exploration was that of literal and metaphysical language-myths in a non-sequential pattern. Alongside that basic structure, but rigidly separated, was the recognition of the practical, metaphoric language of socially constructed speech performed and designed to promote adjustment and facilitate coping. Although recognizing the power of metaphoric language, U3A members were also suspicious of it. Hence their resounding refraining from life-histories, life-review, and reminiscing. Instead, members invested a great deal of intellectual energy in the demetaphorization of experience and in depersonalizing it. This could perhaps be translated as a subversive act, since it was the metaphoric language of life-reviewing that represented the authorized version of the aged self under the gaze of middle-aged society. The result was that the two master types of discourse—the literal (including metaphysical) and the metaphoric—were made to no longer inform each other.

It is also interesting to note that these two modes of articulation were constituted through diametrically opposite logical procedures. While literal discourse was a consequence of decipherment, decodification, and ultimately deduction, the metaphoric was a matter for interpretation supported by induction. In other words, as the former assumed the concealed presence of something—idea, form, myth, event—to be unearthed and made explicit, the latter was based on accumulated evidence of no intrinsic value, whose only justification was considered to be its usefulness.

Systematically and meticulously, all possible bridges between the two modes of articulation were removed to avert any emergence of an overarching narrative that could interlink middle-age symbols and "real" (old age) essentials, or myths.[13] With the absence of feasible metacommunicative facilities, the two modes of articulation provided access to two contrasting realities dominated by two different systems of signification: that of the old as a person impregnated with the world of the essential and the immutable, and that of the person as old, subjected to change, erosion, and coercion. The former—the mind—was free of externally imposed forces, while the latter—the body—was subjected to the dictates of the bio-politics of society, treating old people according to their corporeal manifestations.[14] In fact, members were engaged in what may be called a politics of signification (Hall 1982), where the freedom of the mind was independent of the handling of the body, and the social discourse about the old was kept at bay from the non-discursive existence of the person.[15] Thus, by denying themselves the possibility of reflecting from one domain onto the other, they might have lost the illusory unification of the self and its

supposedly desirable integration,[16] but they might have gained an emanci-
pation of their visceral being. Removing the concern with visibility (see
chapter 3 and chapter 10, n. 1) and acceptability to the realm of appearances and representations blunts the management of the body and of its
social standing and renders it less problematic and frustrating.

The abandonment of the security of the illusory unitary self enabled
members to explore the possibilities of multiple lives[17] without the socially expected imperative of reintegration. The selfless age that was generated was capable of freely travelling between need and desire, practical
reasoning and idealistic formulation. The evident indulgence with humanness and the abolition of boundaries was the choice of the moment and
empowered members to submerge into a general lack of classification
rather than contend with loss of status and social roles. They did, however,
retain the option of a recourse to the world of pragmatism at will and when
necessary. The position of no distinction, coupled with the absence of
social control,[18] placed members on a transient turf of open-ended possibilities, where social distinctions are not amenable to be transformed into
human capital (cf. Bourdieu 1984) and hence do not undergo a process of
commodification, which, in turn, would render them objects of their own
discourse. In a way it could be construed as yet another anticipatory step
towards imminent deterioration in members' conditions. Being human
was no longer conditional upon cultural, contextual considerations but
was "a thing in itself." Facing a possibility of a future state of anticipatory
dehumanization by entering the daunting "fourth age," members had the
self-assurance of subscribing to the language of essential humanness without subjugating it to the interference of the practice of turning old people
into obsolete objects (e.g. Henry 1963:392-474). However, by depriving
society of a meta-narrative about old age, the processing of old people into
objects could not be supported. As is often the case, a set of culturally
induced self-presentations by the aged projects dependency, fecklessness,
and confusion.

Notwithstanding the contrived breach in communication between the
two modes of articulation, some leeway for quantum leaps from one to
the other was apportioned. That was the genetics of myth, which, through
mutation and sudden inexplicable transformation, could bring about
changes in paradigms. The dismissal of progress and history as the driving
forces behind process and the adoption of mutation as the unpredictable
agent of transformation could account for the occurrence of change without committing it to a linear-teleological course. By implication, it also
gave old people the license to use forms of expressions and construct
utterances that do not conform to conventional rules of interpersonal communication. The blend of various historical periods, the resurgence of
myths and memories seemingly not even remotely germane to the conver-

sations, the anachronistic presentation of events and the apparently tenuous rapport between speakers were all allowed within the framework of the rules of mutation and as manifestations of the presence of the thing in itself, not necessarily interlinked with other utterable essentials.

What might be seen as a theatre of the absurd to some, or worse still, as yet another testimony to the scourges of senescence, was merely a pattern of conveying ideas in accordance with the code of the existential state of the speakers. We may thus regard the meetings of the U3A members as providing the setting and the drive for what Dell Hymes has generally termed as a "communicative event" (1962:24–38; 1964:13–25; 1967; 1972:56–70), and our inquiry may therefore be considered as an "ethnography of communication," albeit a somewhat unconventional one.

The linguistic code of the social world of the U3A, and its derived verbal behaviour as performed by members throughout their quest for pure structures and first principles, spells a unique situation. The everyday flow of communication—with the exception of the proscribed cultural spaces for the arts, madness, the mentally disturbed, and the old—is far removed from that code. Interactional expectations to formulate a coherent, intelligible message do not take into account an alternative arrangement of utterances whose acknowledgement might be perilous to the taken-for-granted ease of glossing over fundamental discrepancies of perception and encoding the world. Moreover, rendering the alternative acceptable could rob society of its legitimacy to claim the power–knowledge nexus and to translate it into terms of control. The risk, therefore, that elderly people take by exposing their alternative language to the scrutiny of the outside world is considerable. In that respect, the enclave of the U3A was a safe-enough experimental ground to test out possibilities, balances of loss and profit, and policies for future survival.

There are many unanswered, arguably unanswerable, questions arising from our discussion. It invokes epistemological issues of the possibility of understanding others in general and elderly people in particular, and it touches upon complex concerns with the meaning(s) of meaning, the contours of experience, human universals versus human diversity, and the central subject of representation and the "real." The experiment in ageing unwittingly or otherwise conducted by members of the Cambridge U3A gave us some clues as to the ways elderly people can relate to such questions and to the relevance of this to their being in the world. It is certainly doubtful whether our findings are representative of other groups of elderly or, indeed, of any other collective human effort. However, the intention of this book was not geared to formulate such generalization, nor was it designed to propose a way of understanding ageing. Rather, it is an attempt to study one response to ageing, which could be instructive and illuminating not in its universality or in its uniqueness, but in its plausibility.

Notwithstanding this caveat, it would seem that some of the analytic properties extracted from this case are present in other studies of old age, even though the authors do not always frame the interpretation of their findings in similar terms. It could be argued that while some scholars resort to viewing their researchees through the language of practice,[19] others focus almost exclusively on the prism of myth and meaning (Myerhoff 1978; Kaufman 1986). In all these ethnographic studies, however, it is evident that the elderly described are preoccupied with essential matters, be they the very mundane need to survive or very sublime existentialist concerns. The reduction of reality to the three basic categories of time, space, and reason seems to constitute a unifying theme threaded through all these studies, thus rendering the elderly undeliberate philosophers of their own lives. A previous study by the author (Hazan 1980), which was also set in England, depicted the behavioural patterns of a socio-economically entirely different group of elderly; yet the resemblance in the construction or deconstruction of those three dimensions is striking. It could indicate that in both cases local knowledge was transcended to form old-age-related general knowledge. It could, however, be interpreted as a superimposed explanatory model, which, unsurprisingly in an anthropological research, is applicable to either field. The acid test for such a hypothesis is the applicability of the argument to other situations and the usefulness of what the analysis has to offer to the understanding of other elderly people or, indeed, persons of all ages.

The two modes of articulation distilled in this book have captured the imagination of scholars in all provinces of thought and, as was suggested before, the bifurcation generated by members was no novelty in itself. The clear-cut split, however, is a direct result of a certain structure of complex society which encourages the indiscernible use of the two modes of expression by the non-aged but expects the elderly to resort to either at one time or another. Notwithstanding the structural determinants for this state, it suggests that it is not old age as such that induces the production of a dual language. Rather, the social space allocated for the elderly in our society conditions and regulates that production. If this is the case, then the question of similar social spaces that are in existence and their linguistic composition is in order.

The anthropological literature apparently identifies such cultural spaces as loci of liminal behaviour constituted by the procedures and properties of rites of passage.[20] These transitional stages, which have been widely researched both in simple and complex settings, are conceptualized to be rituals and, indeed, possess many seeming trappings of that category of social events. For many reasons our case could be subsumed under that class, too—it is transitory, preparing its incumbents for things to come. However, it ostensibly lacks any ritualistic elements that could provides it with a metacommunicative bridge between the "dreamt-of" and the "lived-in," as rituals usually do. Yet we are informed by ethnographers of such rituals that communication among novices is either suppressed or confined to the language of mythical essentials, an observation that is commensurate with our findings. It would appear that such situations whose customary labelling brands them as "rituals," could be considered analogous to the case of the experiment in ageing. As such, they can be located in numerous walks of life throughout the life course. The behaviour of members, therefore, drew on past experience, and it was hardly surprising that the model of the boarding-school frequently emerged in their texts. In this sense, it could be suggested that the experiment in ageing is not restricted to the later years, but is part and parcel of our cumulative, albeit disjointed, testing of the relationship between the essential and the practical throughout the life-course.

Concentrating mainly on problems of visibility of the old in society, we tend to lose sight of unobservable behaviour that under the terms of reference suggested in this book is just as important. At the beginning the book considered the question of the audibility of the aged, which, unlike visibility, does not imply integration and participation in society. It is hoped that despite the linguistic contradictions embedded in the experiment in ageing studied in this book, its initiations are rendered audible and intelligible, even though they may have remained willingly invisible. After all, the entrenchment in the principle of the two mutually exclusive modes of articulation came to establish that things are not what they seem to be, and appearances can be deceiving.

A final note must be made in the guise of a methodological admonition. The issue of audibility does not draw on the distinction between the subjective and the intersubjective. The language of the essential and the non-representational forms is not a solipsist enterprise, but a joint production of a peer-group generating a text. The assumed subjective is exposed as intersubjective within a setting that allows individuals to have their views mutually reinforced and formulated. Whether the origin of that consensus is rooted in some kind of collective unconsciousness or is the result of negotiation is beyond the scope of this discussion. However, it is more encouraging to lean on the premise that it is potentially possible to have some access to the language of the old rather than to resort to the comforting but ineffectual conception attributing to the aged extreme individuation, consisting of personal life review and withdrawal into a subjective universe.

Such superimposed subjectivity is an example of the confusion and misunderstanding that might be caused by the incongruity between languages about ageing and the languages of the aged. Reflecting on such discrepancies in communication, it could be argued that the reason for misreading the aged is mistaking texts of non-representation produced by elderly people for the abandoned language of metaphor and symbolic interpretation. It is not uncommon to witness acts of reconstruction by the non-aged aiming at narrating orderly and "meaningful" life stories and reminiscences related by the aged. Such attempts of using a misplaced language to describe the experience of ageing often cannot be handled and are hence ignored or labelled as "pathological," a-chronological, disjointed, and repetitive utterances. An understanding of such aberrations from the expected course of self-presentation could nonetheless be better understood and credited as "normal" if the language of form is employed as an appropriate perspective for framing ageing. This, however, can only be accomplished if audible text replaces the assumed observable context of continuity and elderly people are addressed either through the a-contextual channel of myth, ideas, and non-referential forms or, alternatively, by relating to immediate context of negotiating needs and conditions of survival. However extreme and outrageous such lessons from the experiment might seem, they might help divert attention from learning about the old in terms of the non-old and consider elderly people on their own terms, even if these terms are so literal that they do not lend themselves to the metaphorical translations we live by. This, indeed, presents both the paradox and the challenge of understanding ageing through the perennial polemics that have been guiding human thought, from the ancient Greek philosophers[21] to the members of the U3A. They had at their linguistic disposal a heavy symbolic capital of metaphors, scientific thought, and methods of reasoning. The decision as to how to utilize it was theirs, and, standing at the juncture of the literal and the metaphoric, they turned to the former while abandoning the latter. Language became a tool for stripping experience from the guises of meaning rather than charging it with further symbolic loads. Presumably, that watershed might lead other elderly people in different directions. The path taken by the members of the U3A, however, was a consequence of their capacity to master equally the three modes of articulation, an option of which others, owing to resources and opportunities, may be deprived. Thus, in a manner parallel to the late poetry of modern poets (see Woodward 1980), the elderly in the U3A have created and devised a unique metaphysical mode of articulation, a language of the "still point of the turning world" (as Eliot would have it in "Burnt Norton"). It is also the language to which Wallace Stevens (1954:510) refers when he describes the state of the "total grandeur at the end" and the "inquisitor of structures" stopping at its threshold:

As if the design of all his words takes form
And frame from thinking and is realized.

Notes

CHAPTER 1

   1. For a discussion, as well as an example, of "othering," see Crapanzano (1980) and Lavie (1991).

   2. For a discussion of "meaning" in old age, see Fontana (1976); Langness & Frank (1981); and Rubinstein (1992).

   3. For a review of educational opportunities in old age at the time of the research, see Midwinter (1982).

   4. For a discussion of the problematics of evaluating learning capacity in old age, see Midwinter (1982:49–70) and Perlmutter (1983).

   5. On linguistic codes and social class, see Bernstein (1971–1975).

   6. For an anthropological analysis of the predominance of such rules in shaping cultural phenomena, see Douglas (1975); Douglas & Isherwood (1978); and Bourdieu (1984; 1990:123–139).

   7. For a structural study of that process, see Philipson (1982).

   8. The issue of ascribing non-aged attributes to the evaluation of the performance of elderly people is widely discussed in the literature; see, e.g., discussions of the widespread stereotype of ageism (Butler 1969); the life-satisfaction scale (Gubrium & Lynott 1983); the learning measuring devices (Midwinter 1982:49–70); and the prevailing stigmatic references (Luken 1987).

9. See De Beauvoir (1975:693–698), who regards habit as both a weary repetition and a kind of crystallization in which "the past (is) brought to life again, the future anticipated."

10. V. Turner's concept of "liminoid" behaviour could be understood within given temporal properties of leisure time (see Turner 1977).

11. This method of sociological inference aiming at eliciting cultural categorization is based on the "grounded theory" approach as developed by Glaser & Strauss (1967) and further elaborated by Strauss (1987).

12. As opposed to Bernstein's (1971–1975) analysis of social class vis-à-vis linguistic codes.

13. Shakespeare's metaphor from *As You Like It* on the seven stages of life has been paraphrased in a variety of ways; the "four ages" is but one (see Lowenthal et al. 1975).

14. A concept developed by Hazan (1980) to define the ambiguous state of the aged in society and applied by Laslett (1989) to the analysis of the emergence of the third age.

15. For example, Kimmel (1974) appeared in numerous editions and reprints.

16. For a discussion of the undesirable effect of interference in comparative learning tests, see Hulicka (1967).

17. See Denie & Young (1984) and Norton (1984) for information on the state of universities for the third age in Britain at the time of the research.

18. The "social world perspective" as formally employed in sociology focuses on the abstract communicational channels through which messages are negotiated in a given arena. Geographical–territorial parameters, formerly a must in community studies, are here given secondary importance, while the focus on personal face-to-face interactions is replaced by structural rules autonomous of their human performers. Shibutani (1955) was the first to consider social worlds as configurations of shared communication in industrial societies where actors are engaged in a web of reference groups imbued with diversifying processes and meanings. Strauss (1961; 1962; 1967; 1978; 1982) further elucidated the theoretical foundations and the analytic properties of the concept and advocated its research potentials. The approach has since been employed as a core idea in numerous studies, such as Becker's (1982) analysis of worlds of art, Unruh's (1983) exploration of the "invisible" lives of the aged, and the author's (Hazan 1990) own ethnography of an urban renewal neighbourhood in Israel.

19. For the distinction between life story and life history, see Bertaux (1981).

20. Any attempt at adhering to the long anthropological tradition of community studies would defeat the object of the current research. For even the less territorially bound approaches of symbolic boundaries (Cohen 1985) or social world perspective (Hazan 1990) might restrict the scope of the study to a concept whose relevance to its subject-matter is dubious.

21. On the abandonment of context in its classic anthropological sense, see Barthes (1977); Levi-Strauss (1978); and a discussion by Strathern (1987).

22. For a discussion of that concept, see Schutz & Luckman (1973).

23. Unlike Kaufman (1986), Frank (1980), Myerhoff (1978a), and many others who implicitly or explicitly assume the integration of the self as a temporal whole, our approach follows Berger, Berger, & Kellner (1973), Lifton (1986), and Ewing

(1990) in treating the concept of "self" as spatially as well as temporally disunified—hence the multiple and unrelated manifestations of a person's life stories.

24. The same methodological rationale was implemented by Cumming & Henry (1961).

25. About narratives vis-à-vis old age, see *Journal of Aging Studies,* 1990, Vol. 1; and Wyatt-Brown (1989).

26. For a discussion of the shift in modern literary criticism from the emphasis once put on the author's intentions to the independent status given to the written text, whose deciphering is accomplished by the reader's (varying) interpretation, see Barthes (1977:142–148), in a piece aptly entitled "The Death of the Author"; Foucault's (1979) article on "What is an Author?"; and also Fish (1980) for a discussion of the "authority" of interpretative communities.

CHAPTER 2

1. For a discussion of human universals and human diversity vis-à-vis the anthropology of ageing, see Amoss & Harrell (1981).

2. The Cohort effect refers to the socio-historic experience common to a certain generational unit which also determines the life cycle of its members (see Elder 1974; 1975; 1982).

3. Such solution is indeed ultimate as it annihilates the presence of the anthropologist altogether from the text. It is interesting to note that Paul Radin insisted that the only acceptable ethnology was the life history, self-told by members of an indigenous society. However, as Carpenter (1972:169) poignantly remarks, those who went to such effort found themselves far removed from the mainstream of anthropology.

4. This distinction echoes Wittgenstein's distinction between "surface grammar" and "depth grammar," where the former is the meaning of a word as employed in a certain sentence—the meaning that immediately captures the ear—and the latter is the meaning of that word in many linguistic contexts—that is, many language games; Wittgenstein's (1953:664) example is the word "know". This comparison is given here not without reason, since it is our conviction that ethno-methodology and ordinary-language philosophy (springing from Wittgenstein's later work) share many parallels, which will be elaborated further.

5. For macro-sociological discussions of the medicalization—the constitution of a subject as an object to the power and knowledge of the medical profession—of the person in modern society, see Zola (1982) and Turner (1984). The case of old age is analysed, for example, by Gubrium (1986); and Arluke & Peterson (1981).

6. A similar method for eliminating age-dependent pathological variables was employed by Cumming & Henry (1961).

7. It should be noted that I use the term "deconstruction" throughout the book in its literal sense—i.e. to describe the shift of the elderly from the metaphorical level into the metonymical as consisting not of a smooth transition but, rather, a sort of breakdown. My use of the term should therefore not be confused with that of Derrida (1967). Indeed, my own analytical perspective regarding the "author-free"

interpretation of texts is rather critical of Derrida's, being in line with "post-deconstructivist" works.

CHAPTER 3

1. For an elaborated discussion of this matter, see Gubrium (1986). The fact that the unclear medical diagnosis of geriatrically related syndromes further encourages its socially prescribed categorization is suggested in J. Gregory's (1978) article, whose apt title is: "Senility as a Synonym for Old Age: Inappropriate Diagnoses in Geriatrics."

2. A concept first introduced into gerontology by Burgess (1950).

3. The concept of "deculturation" in relation to old age was formulated by Anderson (1972).

4. A concept propounded by Marshall (1979) to propose that "no future lies beyond the passage, only the passage and its termination become relevant" (p. 351).

5. An application of the concept of anomie to the understanding of old age can be found in Fontana (1976).

6. The theory of disengagement was developed by Cumming & Henry (1961).

7. Symbolic invisibility is a concept suggested by Myerhoff (1978a) to describe the social disregard of the aged.

8. See Myerhoff & Simic (1978); with regard to visibility and performance, see Myerhoff (1982).

9. This notion, introduced by Erikson (1959) and elaborated within the field of developmental psychology, is continually under epistemological criticism (McCulloch 1980). Other critical questions involve the cultural construction of that very notion (Brandstadter 1990) as well as the social construction of the person (Shweder & Miller 1985). These two issues, emphasized and articulated in many anthropological studies, join forces with novel approaches in psychology that seek to replace the Eriksonian linear, universal, and deterministic conception by a multi-dimensional model. Indeed, the anthropological conviction that what we regard as a "person" is in fact a bricolage of selves that do not intrinsically relate (see Carrithers, Collins, & Lukes 1985; Ewing 1990) precludes the possibility of a strict and linear personal development.

10. The idea that cultural themes can be used as the basis for the understanding of old age is found in Kaufman (1981). It should be emphasized that these "themes"—whatever their validity may be—constitute not a literal but a metaphoric language that—according to our line of argument—does not play a dominant part in the life of the old.

11. See, e.g., Sperber's (1975) arguments regarding the metonymical system of symbolism in which the "thing-in-itself" carries with it its own truth value.

12. For studies of linguistic socialization combining word and action, see the classical works of Bernstein (1971–1975), as well as Hymes (1974) for the over-arching theoretical approach. Particular case studies can be found in the studies of Garnica & King (1979) and Katriel (1986).

13. Eliseo Veron (1990:176) has argued, following Bateson (1964), that metonymy is indeed the "couch" of all production of sense, the primary level of signification, surfaced by the iconic level, which can transform it into metaphor.

14. Kathleen Woodward, in her study of the late poems of Eliot, Pound, Stevens, and Williams, argues that ageing puts the poet in a position to see "the whole of the system": "The wisdom of these four poets inheres in their having recognized, and accepted, the 'other,' that was always stranger to their work . . . it is characterized, above all, by humility . . . that contradicts the Western way of thinking about mankind in the world—imperialism over nature and other people" (Woodward 1980:8, 15, 172).

15. The linguistic categories of literal, metaphoric, contextual, and metaphysical echo Bateson's distinction between what he calls "Learning I, II and III"—the logical categories of learning and communication (Bateson 1972:279–309). Endowing the notion of "context" with a prominent function in this hierarchical distinction, Bateson sets out to describe, in a manner very similar to our own, Learning I as "analogic, habituated, and contextual"; Learning II as characterized by the ability to "devise the context" ("learning to learn"); and Learning III as "reconstructing the context—recreating Learning II," a rare ability, which, says Bateson, "does occur from time to time in psychotherapy, religious conversion, and in other sequences in which there is profound reorganization of character." As for the next stage in this hierarchy, Language IV, Bateson comments that it "does not occur on this Earth."

16. "Episteme" is the term coined by Foucault (1970) in order to express a relativistic conception of the overall prevailing assumptions that constitute the framework of knowledge and what is to be accounted as knowledge in a given historical epoch. Thus, the "episteme" of the Renaissance, to quote only one famous example, is different from that of the Middle Ages with respect to its view of man's place in nature.

CHAPTER 4

1. For an anthropological discussion of this concept, see Sahlins (1976).

2. For a description of such "experiments" in human socialization, see Shattuck (1981).

3. For an interpretation of jokes in this vein, see Douglas (1975:90–114).

CHAPTER 5

1. A large part of the gerontological discourse can be seen to revolve around the two alternatives defined as "discontinuity" and "continuity". The former suggests that ageing could be defined as a major break—or "disengagement"—that precedes death (Cumming & Henry 1961; Anderson 1972; Burgess 1950), while the latter proposes that it could be characterized as a stage in which consciousness of death brings about integration and continuity of the life course (Butler 1963, Myerhoff 1978a, 1978b, 1984; Unruh 1983; Kaufman 1986). In this way, ageing is circumscribed to the individual and his/her ability to cope with or transcend old age.

2. The symbolic perpetuation of one's social presence is a much-discussed subject in the behavioural sciences; see, e.g., Becker's (1973) notion of the hero culture as a denial of death, Lifton's (1977;1983) concept of symbolic immortality, and Bauman's discussion in the strive for immortality (Bauman 1992).

CHAPTER 6

1. For a discussion of the meaning of social space vs. physical environment in old age, see Rowles (1978) and Rowles & Ohta (1981).

CHAPTER 7

1. Following ethnomethodological rather than phenomenological tradition (for the fundamental difference, see Rogers 1983), this chapter seeks to unravel the rules underlying the descriptive activity under study. Such rules are constantly present in the text and constitute a self-referent language testifying to the textual place within a given discourse. For a discussion of such a method, see Garfinkel (1967) and the ensuing extensive controversy in the relevant literature.

2. For a discussion of the relevance of phenomenological assumptions to the understanding of the images of ageing and its concomitant social interaction, see Philibert (1984).

3. In a manner quite analogous to that described as part of the "modernist condition" in Berger, Berger, & Kellner's (1973) *The Homeless Mind.*

4. A linguistically based concept ("phonemics") indicating the researchees' terminology whereby their world-view is constructed. The counter-term "etic" ("phonetics") indicates the researcher's analytic model relating to the field under study. The terms were coined by Pike (1954).

5. Notably some versions of semiotics (see, e.g., Barthes 1976) and the so-called post-modern trend (see, e.g., Foster 1985).

CHAPTER 8

1. The distinction between "duration" (a meaningful flow of time) and "sequence" (any consecutive chain of events) was developed by Luscher (1974).

2. This is contrary to the common belief that the elderly tend to dwell on the past (see Hazan 1980).

CHAPTER 9

1. The assumption that the elderly in Western society are socially invisible and hence strive for visibility was propounded by Myerhoff (1978a; 1982). A preassumption of the need for means of reflexivity underlies this argument (see chapters 1 and 3).

CHAPTER 10

1. An extreme case of such representation is described by Kunda (1992).

2. The programme of studies addressed and analysed here was prepared and devised at the time of the research but took effect during the following academic year.

3.   This observation stands in apparent contradiction to Myerhoff's abundance of drama and ritual in the world of the elderly (Myerhoff 1977a; 1978b; 1984). A possible explanation for this discrepancy could be offered in terms of our analysis to the effect that the ceremonial properties in the behaviour of the aged as explored by Myerhoff reflect a contextual language disguised as a metaphorical one (see chapter 11). This ritualistic visibility could be construed as a pragmatic reaction to the expectation by the non-old for dramatic displays of the old relating to fertility, identity, life and death, and other existential issues attributed to this cultural category by society. Support to this argument can be found in the process of cultural "learning to act old" as described by Hendricks (1992). The symbolic roles assumed by the elderly in different societies (Turnbull 1984:229; Cool & McCabe 1983) might provide further testimony.

CHAPTER 11

1.   The enactment of life stories as a means of constructing a sense of continuity and identity among the aged was studied and encouraged by Myerhoff (1982). Hazan (1987) describes a seemingly similar phenomenon but argues that it must be understood in terms of responding to contextual conditions rather than as a meaning-searching device.

2.   For example, the significance of altruistic caring and the importance of "giving something for nothing" (Titmuss 1970; Gouldner 1975:260–99).

3.   For discussions of that theoretical position, see Gubrium and Buckholdt (1977). For an example of popular construction of child's development, see Brandtstadter (1990).

4.   For such an implied approach, see Myerhoff (1978b); Langness & Frank (1981); Frank & Vanderburgh (1986); and Kaufman (1986).

5.   For the distinction "writerly" vs. "readerly" texts, see Barthes (1977).

6.   The concept of "local knowledge" being the foundation of the context-bound tenets in anthropological inquiry (Geertz 1983) presupposes, not unlike semiological approaches, an overall inter-connectedness of cultural texts.

7.   For a discussion of the theatrical properties of the practice of descriptive activity, see Gubrium, Buckholdt, & Lynott (1982).

8.   Following Said's exhortation in "Orientalism" (Said 1978).

9.   For a discussion of these problematics in anthropological research, see Pels and Nancel (1991).

10.   See Manheimer's (1989) analysis of this distinction.

11.   This does not suggest a sense of "symbolic immortality" (Lifton 1977) but a construction of "transversal continuity" (Hazan 1985).

12.   On the problem of representation in anthropological thought, see Marcus & Fischer (1986) and Clifford & Marcus (1986); also see discussion in chapter 2.

13.   The analytic difference between "symbol" or "metaphor" and myth adopted in this discussion is based on Leach (1976). The transformation from the former to the latter is analysed by Rossi (1983).

14.   For a discussion of Foucault's conception of "bio-politics," see Hewitt (1991).

15. Foucault's notion of non-discursive practices is embedded in many of his writings and ought to be understood in terms of the productive and reproductive nexus between power and knowledge (Foucault 1980).

16. Erikson's notion of the development of the self through the life course can be adduced to exemplify this assumption (Erickson 1959; 1982).

17. For the sociological perspective of the concept of "life-worlds," see Luckman (1970); Schutz & Luckman (1973).

18. In terms used by M. Douglas (1970; 1978), this combination can be identified as a "low-grid" (loose classification) and "low-group" (loose control) position.

19. The anthropological literature on ageing is rife with such studies. From Simmons (1945), who compared the socio-economic circumstances of the aged in different "primitive" societies, to modern ethnographers of the condition of the old in contemporary Western society (Vesperi 1985; Sokolovsky & Cohen 1981; Eckert 1980; Francis 1984), researchers have sought to document the practical dimension of late life.

20. For an analytic description of rites of passage, see Van-Gennep [1960 (1908)]; Turner (1969).

21. For a discussion of the relevance of this issue to anthropological thought, see Lloyd (1990).

Bibliography

Amoss, P. T., & Harrell, S. (Eds.) (1981). *Other Ways of Growing Old: Anthropological Perspectives.* Stanford, CA: Stanford University Press.

Anderson, B. (1972). The Process of Deculturation—Its Dynamics Among United States Aged. *Anthropological Quarterly, 45*: 209–216.

Apple, M. W. (Ed.) (1982). *Cultural and Economic Reproduction in Education.* London: Routledge.

Arluke, A., & Peterson, J. (1981). Accidental Medicalization of Old Age and Its Social Control Implications. In L. Fry (Ed.), *Dimensions: Aging, Culture and Health* (pp. 271–284). New York: J.F. Bergin.

Asad, T. (1986). The Concept of Cultural Translation in British Social Anthropology. In J. Clifford & G. Marcus (Eds.), *Writing Culture: The Poetics and Politics of Ethnography.* Berkeley, CA: University of California Press.

Astington, J. (1991). Narrative and the Child's Theory of Mind. In B. Britton & A. Pellegrini (Eds.), *Narrative Thought and Narrative Language.* Hillsdale, NJ: Lawrence Erlbaum.

Austin, J. L. (1962). *How to Do Things with Words.* London: Oxford University Press.

Barthes, R. (1976). *Writing Degree Zero and Elements of Semiology* (trans. A. Lavers & C. Smith). Boston, MA: Beacon Press.

Barthes, R. (1977). *Image, Music, Text.* London: Fontana.

Bass, S. A. (1987). University and Community Partnership: Developing Link-ages for Quality Gerontological Training and Institutional Expansion. *Educational Gerontology,* 13: 307–324.

Bateson, G. (1972). The Logical Categories of Language and Communication. In *Steps to an Ecology of Mind* (pp. 279–309). San Francisco, CA: Chandler Publishing Company.

Bateson, G., & Jackson, D. D. (1964). Some Varieties of Pathogenic Organiza-tion. *Disorders of Communication,* 42: 270–290.

Bauman, Z. (1992). *Mortality and Immortality and Other Life Strategies.* Cam-bridge, U.K.: Polity Press.

Becker, E. (1962). *The Birth and Death of Meaning.* New York: The Free Press.

Becker, E. (1973). *The Denial of Death.* New York: The Free Press.

Becker, H. (1982). *Art Worlds.* Berkeley, CA: University of California Press.

Berger, P., & Luckman, T. (1967). *The Social Construction of Reality: A Treatise in the Sociology of Knowledge.* Garden City, NY: Anchor Books.

Berger, P., Berger, B., & Kellner, H. (1973). *The Homeless Mind.* New York: Random House; Vintage.

Bernardi, B. (1985). *Age Class Systems: Social Institutions and Politics Based on Age.* Cambridge, U.K.: Cambridge University Press.

Bernstein, B. (1971–75). *Class, Codes and Control.* London: Routledge & Kegan Paul.

Bernstein, B. (1977). Foreword. In D. S. Adlam, G. H. Turner, & L. Lineker (Eds.), *Code in Context.* London: Routledge.

Bernstein, B. (1990). *Class, Codes and Control.* Vol. IV: *The Structuring of Pedagogic Discourse.* London: Routledge.

Bertaux, D. (Ed.) (1981). *Biography and Society: The Life History Approach in the Social Sciences.* London: Sage Publications.

Birren, J. E., & Munnichs, M. A. (1983). General Introduction. In J. E. Birren, M. A. Munnichs, et al. (Eds.), *Aging: A Challenge to Science and Society,* Vol. 3: *Behavioural Sciences* (pp. 3–5). Oxford, U.K.: Oxford University Press.

Blythe, R. (1979). *The View in Winter.* New York: Harcourt Brace Jovanovich.

Bourdieu, P. (1984). *Distinctions.* Cambridge, MA: Harvard University Press.

Bourdieu, P. (1990). *In Other Words: Essays Towards a Reflexive Anthropol-ogy.* Cambridge, U.K.: Polity Press.

Bourdieu, P., & Passeron, J. C. (1970). *La Reproduction: éléments pour une théorie du système d'enseignement.* Paris: Minuit. (Trans. R. Nice, as *Reproduction in Education, Society and Culture.* Beverly Hills, CA: Sage Publications, 1977.)

Bowles, N. L., & Poon, L. W. (1985). *Age and Semantic Context Effects in Lexical Decisions.* Paper presented at the Annual Meeting of the East-ern Psychological Association, Boston, MA.

Brandtstadter, J. (1990). Development as a Personal and Cultural Construction. In G. Semin & K. Gergen (Eds.), *Everyday Understanding* (pp. 83–129). London: Sage Publications.

Bromley, D. (1974). *The Psychology of Human Aging* (2nd edition). Harmondsworth, U.K.: Penguin.

Bunge, R. (1984). *An American Urphilosopie: American Philosophy BP (Before Pragmatism)*. Washington, DC: University Press of America, Lanham.

Burgess, E. (1950). Personal and Social Adjustment in Old Age. In M. Derber (Ed.), *The Aged and Society* (pp. 138–156). Champaign, IL: Industrial Relations Research Association.

Butler, R. N. (1963). The Life Review: An Interpretation of Reminiscence among the Aged. *Psychiatry, 26*: 65–76.

Butler, R. N. (1969). Age-ism: Another Form of Bigotry. *The Gerontologist, 9*: 243–246.

Butler, R. N. (1970). Looking Forward to What? The Life Review, Lacacy and Excessive Identity vs. Change. *American Behavioral Scientist, 14*: 121–128.

Carey, J. (1987). Walter Benjamin, Marshall McLuhan and the Emegence of Visual Society. *Prospects, 11*: 29–38.

Carpenter, E. (1972). *Oh, What a Blow That Phantom Gave Me!* London: Paladin Books.

Carrithers, M., Collins, S., & Lukes, S. (Eds.) (1985). *The Category of the Person*. Cambridge, U.K.: Cambridge University Press.

Caplan, P. (1988). Engendering Knowledge: The Politics of Ethnography. *Anthropology Today, 4* (5): 8–12; *4* (6): 14–17.

Chomsky, N. (1966). *Cartesian Linguistics*. New York: Harper & Row.

Chomsky, N. (1975). *Reflections on Language*. New York: Pantheon.

Cicourel, A. (1972). Basic and Normative Rules in the Negotiation of Status and Role. In D. Sudnow (Ed.), *Studies in Social Interaction* (pp. 229–258). New York: The Free Press.

Clifford, J. (1983). On Ethnographic Authority. *Representations, 1* (2): 118–146.

Clifford, J. (1986). On Ethnographic Allegory. In J. Clifford & G. E. Marcus (Eds.), (1986). *Writing Culture: The Poetics and Politics of Ethnography* (pp. 98–121). Berkeley, CA: University of California Press.

Clifford, J., & Marcus, G. E. (Eds.), (1986). *Writing Culture: The Poetics and Politics of Ethnography*. Berkeley, CA: University of California Press.

Cohen, A. P. (1985). *Symbolic Construction of Community*. London: Tavistock.

Cohen-Shalev, A. (1989). Old Age Style: Developmental Changes in Creative Production from a Life-Span Perspective. *Journal of Aging Studies, 3* (1): 21–39.

Cohen-Shalev, A. (1992). Self and Style: The Development of Artistic Expression from Youth through Midlife to Old Age in the Works of Henrik Ibsen. *Journal of Aging Studies, 6* (3): 289–301.

Cool, L., & McCabe, J. (1983). The Scheming Hag and the "Dear Old Thing": the Anthropology of Aging Women. In J. Sokolovsky (Ed.), *Growing Old in Different Societies* (pp. 56–71). Belmont, CA: Wadsworth.

Coupland, J., & Coupland, N. (1991). Formulating Age: Dimensions of Age Identity in Elderly Talk. *Discourse Processes, 14*: 87–106.

Coupland, N. (Ed.) (1988). *Styles of Discourse.* London: Croom Helm.

Coupland, N., Coupland, J., & Giles, H. (Eds.) (1991). Ageing and Society. *Sociolinguistic Issues in Ageing. Special Issue, Vol. 11* (2).

Coupland, N., & Nussbaum, J. (Eds.) (1993). *Life Span Discourse and Social Identity.* Beverly Hills, CA: Sage Publications.

Craik, F. I. M., & Byrd, M. (1982). Aging and Cognitive Deficits: The Role of Attentional Resources. In F. I. M. Craik & S. E. Trehub (Eds.), *Aging and Cognitive Processes.* New York: Plenum Press.

Crapanzano, V. (1980). *Tuhami: Portrait of a Moroccan.* Chicago, IL: University of Chicago Press.

Cumming, E., & Henry, W. (1961). *Growing Old: The Process of Disengagement.* New York: Basic Books.

Davidson, D. (1979). On Metaphor. In S. Sachs (Ed.), *On Metaphor.* Chicago, IL: University of Chicago Press.

de Beauvoir, S. (1975). *The Coming of Age.* New York: Warner Communications.

Denie, J., & Young, M. (1984). Major Influences on U3A Universities. In E. Midwinter (Ed.), *Mutual Aid Universities* (pp. 91–104). London: Croom Helm.

Derrida, J. (1967). *Of Grammatology.* Baltimore, MD: Johns Hopkins University Press.

Douglas, M. (1970). *Natural Symbols: Explorations in Cosmology.* New York: Pantheon Books.

Douglas, M. (1975). *Implicit Meanings.* London: Routledge & Kegan Paul.

Douglas, M. (1978). *Cultural Bias.* Occasional Paper no. 35. London: Royal Anthropological Institute of Great Britain and Ireland.

Douglas, M., & Isherwood, B. (1978). *The World of Goods.* New York: Basic Books.

Dubois, E. E. (1975). Adult Education and Andragogy: New Opportunities for the Aging. In M. Spencer & C. Dorr (Eds.), *Understanding Aging: A Multidisciplinary Approach* (pp. 179–195). New York: Appleton-Century-Crofts; Prentice-Hall.

Eckert, J. K. (1980). *The Unseen Elderly.* San Diego, CA: Campanile Press.

Elder, G. H., Jr. (1974). *Children of the Great Depression.* Chicago, IL: University of Chicago Press.

Elder, G. H., Jr. (1975). Age Differentiation and Life Course. *Annual Review of Sociology I.* Palo Alto, CA: Annual Reviews.

Elder, G. H., Jr. (1982). Historical Experiences in the Later Years. In T. K. Harevers & K. J. Adams (Eds.), *Ageing and Life Course Transitions: An Interdisciplinary Perspective* (pp. 75–108). London: Tavistock.

Erickson, E. (1959). Identity and the Life Cycle. *Psychological Issues, 1*: 1.

Erickson, E. (1982). *The Life Cycle Completed.* New York: W. W. Norton.

Ewen, S, & Ewen, E. (1982). *Channels of Desire.* New York: McGraw-Hill.

Ewing, K. P. (1990). The Illusion of Wholeness: Culture, Self and the Experience of Inconsistency. *Ethos, 18*: 251–278.

Fabian, J. (1983). *Time and the Other: How Anthropology Makes Its Object.* New York: Columbia University Press.

Featherstone, M. & Hepworth, M. (1990). Images of Aging. In J. Bond & P. G. Coleman (Eds.), *Ageing in Society: An Introduction to Social Gerontology.* London: Sage Publications.

Featherstone, M., & Hepworth, M. (1991). The Mask of Ageing and the Post-Modern Life Course. In: M. Featherstone, M. Hepworth, & B. Turner (Eds.), *The Body: Social Process and Cultural Theory* (pp. 370–389). London: Sage Publications.

Fish, S. (1980). *Is There a Text in This Class?—The Authority of Interpretive Communities.* Cambridge, MA: Harvard University Press.

Fontana, A. (1976). *The Last Frontier.* Beverly Hills, CA: Sage Publications.

Foster, H. (Ed.) (1985). *Postmodern Culture.* London: Pluto.

Foucault, M. (1979). What is an Author? (trans. K. Hanet). *Screen, XX* (1): 13–33.

Foucault, M. (1980). *Power/Knowledge: Selected Interviews and Other Writings.* Brighton, U.K.: Harvester Press.

Francis, D. (1984). *Will you Still Need Me, Will You Still Feed Me When I'm 84?* Bloomington, IN: Indiana University Press.

Frank, G. (1980). Life Histories in Gerontology: The Subjective Side of Aging. In C. L. Fry & J. Keith (Eds.), *New Methods for Old Age Research: Anthropological Alternatives* (pp. 155–176). Chicago, IL: Loyola University Press.

Frank, G., & Vanderburgh, R. M. (1986). Cross-Cultural Use of Life-History Methods in Gerontology. In C. Fry & J. Keith (Eds.), *New Methods for Old Age Research: Strategies for Studying Diversity* (pp. 185–212). New York: Bergin & Garvey.

Friedman, J. (1987). Prolegomena to the Adventures of Phallus in Blunderland: An Anti-Anti-Discourse. *Culture and History, 1* (1): 31–49.

Futerman, V. (1984). The University of the Third Age in Cambridge. In E. Midwinter (Ed.), *Mutual Aid Universities* (Chapter 8). London: Croom Helm.

Garfinkel, H. (1967). *Studies in Ethnomethodology.* Engelwood-Cliffs, NJ: Prentice Hall.

Garnica, O., & King, M. (Eds.), (1979). *Language, Children and Society.* Oxford, U.K.: Pergamon.

Geertz, C. (1966). Religion as a Cultural System. In M. Barton (Ed.), *Anthropological Approaches to the Study of Religion* (pp. 1–46). London: Tavistock.

Geertz, C. (1983). *Local Knowledge: Further Essays in Interpretive Anthropology.* New York: Basic Books.

Gellner, E. (1973). *Cause and Meaning in the Social Sciences.* London: Routledge & Kegan Paul.

Giddens, A. (1991). *Modernity and Self-identity: Self and Society in the Late Modern Age.* Cambridge, U.K.: Polity Press.

Giles, H., & Robinson, P. (Eds.) (1990). *Handbook of Language and Social Psychology.* Chichester, U.K.: Wiley.

Giles, H., Williams, A., & Coupland, N. (1990). Communication, Health and the Elderly: Frameworks, Agenda, and a Model. In: H. Giles, N.

Coupland, & J. M. Wiemann (Eds.), *Communication, Health and the Elderly* (pp. 1–128). London: Manchester University Press.

Glaser, B., & Strauss, A. (1967). *The Discovery of Grounded Theory*. Chicago, IL: Aldine.

Goethe, J. W. (1954) {1790}. *Faust* (trans. Sir T. Martin). London: Dent.

Goody, J. (1977). *The Domestication of the Savage Mind*. Cambridge, U.K.: Cambridge University Press.

Gouldner, A. (1975). *For Sociology: Renewal and Critique in Sociology Today*. London: Penguin.

Greer, G. (1991). *The Change: Women, Ageing and Menopause*. London: Hamish Hamilton.

Gregory, J. (1978). Senility as a Synonym for Old Age: Inappropriate Diagnoses in Geriatrics. In H. Schwartz, & C. Kart (Eds.), *Dominant Issues in Medical Sociology* (pp. 86–90). Boston, MA: Addison-Wesley.

Gubrium, J. F. (1973). *The Myth of the Golden Years: A Socio-Environmental Theory of Aging*. Springfield, IL: Charles C Thomas.

Gubrium, J. F. (1986). *Oldtimers and Alzheimer's: The Descriptive Organization of Senility*. Greenwich, CT: JAI Press.

Gubrium, J. F. (1994). *Speaking of Lives*. New York: Aldine de Gruyter.

Gubrium, J. F., & Buckholdt, D. R. (1977). *Toward Maturity: The Social Processing of Human Development*. San Francisco, CA: Jossey-Bass.

Gubrium, J. F, Buckholdt, D. R., & Lynott, R. J. (1982). Considerations of a Theory of Descriptive Activity. *Mid-American Review of Sociology, 7*: 17–35.

Gubrium, J. F., & Lynott, R. S. (1983). Rethinking Life Satisfaction. *Human Organization, 42*: 30–38.

Hall, S. (1982). The Rediscovery of Ideology: The Return of the Repressed in Media Studies. In M. Gurevitch, T. Bennett, & J. Woollacott, *Culture, Society and the Media* (pp. 56–90). London: Methuen.

Handelman, D. (1990). *Models and Mirrors*. Cambridge, U.K.: Cambridge University Press.

Havighurst, R. J. (1954). Flexibility and Social Roles of the Aged. *American Journal of Sociology, 1* (4): 309–313.

Havighurst, R. J. (1963). Successful Aging. In R. H. Williams, C. Tibbitts, & W. Donahue (Eds.), *Processes of Aging,* Vol. I. New York: Atherton Press.

Havighurst, R. J. (1975). The Future Aged: The Use of Time and Money. *Gerontologist, 15*: 10–15.

Hazan, H. (1980). *The Limbo People: A Study of the Constitution of the Time Universe Among the Aged*. London: Routledge and Kegan Paul.

Hazan, H. (1984). Religion in an Old-Age Home—Symbolic Adaptation as Survival Strategy. *Ageing and Society, 4*: 137–156.

Hazan, H. (1985). Continuity and Transformation among the Aged: A Study in the Anthropology of Time. *Current Anthropology, 35*: 367–378.

Hazan, H. (1986). Body Image and Temporality among the Aged: A Case Study of an Ambivalent Symbol. *Studies in Symbolic Interaction,* Vol. 7 (Part A, pp. 305–329). Greenwich, CT: JAI Press.

Hazan, H. (1987). Myth into Reality: Enacting Life Histories in an Institutional Setting. In: G. L. Maddox & E. W. Busse (Eds.), *Aging—The Universal Human Experience* (pp. 441–448). New York: Springer.

Hazan, H. (1990). *A Paradoxical Community.* Greenwich, CT: JAI Press.

Hazan, H. (1992). *Managing Change in Old Age.* New York: State University of New York Press.

Hazan, H. (1994). *Old Age: Construction and Deconstructions.* Cambridge, U.K.: Cambridge University Press.

Hazan, H. (1994). Lost Horizons Regained: Old Age and the Anthropology of Contemporary Society. In: A. S. Ahmed & C. N. Shore (Eds.), *The Future of Anthropology* (pp. 203–227). London: Athlone.

Heidegger, M. (1962). *Being and Time* (trans. J. Macquarrie & E. Robinson). New York: Harper & Row.

Heilman, S. (1976). *Synagogue Life: A Study in Symbolic Interaction.* Chicago, IL: Chicago University Press.

Heilman, S. (1983). *The People of the Book.* Chicago, IL: Chicago University Press.

Hendricks, J. (1992). Learning to Act Old: Heroes, Villains or Old Fools. *Journal of Aging Studies, 6*: 1–12.

Henry, J. (1963). *Culture Against Man.* New York: Random House.

Hepworth, M., & Featherstone, M. (1982). *Surviving Middle Age.* Oxford: Blackwell.

Hepworth, M., & Featherstone, M. (1991). The Mask of Ageing and the Postmodern Life Course. In: M. Featherstone, M. Hepworth, & B. S. Turner (Eds.), *The Body: Social Process and Cultural Theory* (pp. 371–389). London: Sage.

Hewitt, M. (1991). Bio-Politica and Social Policy: Foucault's Account of Welfare. In: M. Featherstone, M. Hepworth, & B. Turner (Eds.), *The Body: Social Process and Cultural Theory* (pp. 370–389). London: Sage Publications.

Hockey, J., & James, A. (1993). *Growing Up and Growing Old: Ageing and Dependency in the Life Course.* London: Sage Publications.

Hulicka, I. M. (1967). Age Differences in Retention as a Function of Interference. *Journal of Gerontology, 22*: 180–184.

Hymes, D. (1962). The Ethnography of Speaking. In T. Gladwin & W. C. Sturtevant (Eds.), *Anthropology and Human Behaviour* (pp. 13–53). Washington, DC: Anthropological Society of Washington.

Hymes, D. (1964). Introduction: Toward Ethnographies of Communication. In J. J. Gumperz & D. Hymes (Eds.), The Ethnography of Communication. *American Anthropologist, 66* (6), Part 2: 1–34.

Hymes, D. (1967). The Anthropology of Communication. In: F. E. X. Dance (Ed.), *Human Communication Theory: Original Essays* (pp. 1–39). New York: Holt, Rinehart and Winston.

Hymes, D. (1972). Models of the Interaction of Language and Social Life. In: J. J. Gumperz & D. Hymes (Eds.), *Directions in Sociolinguistics: The Ethnography of Communication* (pp. 35–71). New York: Holt, Rinehart and Winston.

Hymes, D. (1974). *Foundations in Sociolinguistics*. Philadelphia, PA: University of Pennsylvania Press.

Jay, M. (1988a). Scopic Regimes of Modernity. In H. Foster (Ed.), *Vision and Visuality* (pp. 3–23). Seattle, WA: Bay Press.

Jay, M. (1988b). The Rise of Hermeneutics and the Crisis of Ocularcentrism. *Poetics Today, 9* (2): 307–326.

Katriel, T. (1986). *Talking Straight: "Dugri" Speech in Israeli Sabra Culture.* Cambridge, U.K.: Cambridge University Press.

Katriel, T. (1991). Sodot: Secret Sharing as a Social Form among Israeli Children. In *Communal Webs* (pp. 183–197). Albany: State University of New York Press.

Kaufman, S. R. (1981). Cultural Components of Identity in Old Age. *Ethos, 9* (1): 51–87.

Kaufman, S. R. (1986). *The Ageless Self: Sources of Meaning in Late Life.* Madison, WI: The University of Wisconsin Press.

Keith, J. (1980). The Best is Yet to Be, Toward an Anthropology of Age. *Annual Review of Anthropology, 9*: 339–364.

Kemper, S. (1986). Imitation of Complex Syntactic Constructions by Elderly Adults. *Applied Psycholinguistics, 7*: 277–287.

Kemper, S. (1988). Geriatric Psycholinguistics: Syntactic Limitations of Oral and Written Language. In L. Light & D. Burke (Eds.), *Language, Memory and Aging* (pp. 58–76). Cambridge, U.K.: Cambridge University Press.

Kertzer, D. & Keith, J. (Eds.), (1984). *Age and Anthropological Theory.* Ithaca, NY: Cornell University Press.

Kimmel, D. C. (1974). *Adulthood and Aging.* New York: John Wiley.

Kline-Taylor, N. (1985). Symbolic Dimensions in Cultural Anthropology. *Current Anthropology, 26*: 167–186.

Koch, K. (1977). *I Never Told Anybody: Teaching Poetry Writing in a Nursing Home.* New York: Random House.

Kunda, G. (1992). *Engineering Culture: Control and Commitment in a Hi-Tech Corporation.* Philadelphia, PA: Temple University Press.

Labouvie-Vief, G. (1980). Adaptive Dimensions in Adult Cognition. In N. Datan, & N. Lohmann (Eds.), *Transitions of Aging* (pp. 3–24). New York: Academic Press.

Labouvie-Vief, G., & Schell, D. A. (1982). Learning and Memory in Later Life. In B. B. Wolman (Ed.), *Handbook of Developmental Psychology.* Engelwood Cliffs, NJ: Prentice-Hall.

Lakoff, G., & Johnson, M. (1980). *Metaphors We Live By.* Chicago, IL: University of Chicago Press.

Lambert, J., Laslett, P., & Clay, H. (1984). *The Image of the Elderly on TV: Report of the Research Committee Project.* Cambridge, U.K.: U3A Cambridge.

Langness, L. L., & Frank, G. (1981). *Lives: An Anthropological Approach to Biography.* Novato, CA: Chandler & Sharp.

Laslett, P. (1984). The Education of Elderly in Britain. In E. Midwinter (Ed.), *Mutual Aid Universities* (pp. 21–50). London: Croom-Helm.

Laslett, P. (1989). *A Fresh Map of Life. The Emergence of the Third Age.* London: Weidenfeld & Nicolson.

Lavie, S. (1991). *The Poetics of Military Occupation.* Berkeley, CA: University of California Press.

Leach, E. (1971). Chronus and Chronos. In *Rethinking Anthropology* (pp. 124–132). London: Athlone Press.

Leach, E. (1976). *Culture and Communication.* Cambridge, U.K.: Cambridge University Press.

Lemon, B. W., et al. (1972). An Explanation of the Activity Theory of Aging: Activity Types and Life Satisfaction among In-Movers to a Retirement Community. *Journal of Gerontology, 27*: 511–523.

Levinson, D., Darrow, C., Klein, E., Levinson, M., & McKee, B. (1978). *The Seasons of Man's Life.* New York: Knopf.

Levi-Strauss, C. (1978). *Myth and Meaning.* London: Routledge.

Lieberman, M. A. (1974). Relocation Research and Social Policy. *The Gerontologist, 14*: 494–501.

Lieberman, M. A., & Tobin, S. S. (1983). *The Experience of Old Age.* New York: Basic Books.

Lifton, R. (1977). The Sense of Immortality. In H. Feifel (Ed.), *New Meanings of Death.* New York: McGraw-Hill.

Lifton, R. (1983). *The Broken Connection.* New York: Basic Books.

Lifton, R. (1986). *The Nazi Doctors.* New York: Basic Books.

Lloyd, G. E. R. (1990). *Demystifying Mentalities.* Cambridge, U.K.: Cambridge University Press.

Loewe, H. (1977). *Lernpsychologie: Einführung des Psychischen.* Stuttgart: Fischer.

Lowenthal, M., et al. (1975). *Four Stages of Life.* San Francisco, CA: Jossey-Bass.

Lubrousky, M. R. (1990). Alchemist's Visions: Cultural Norms in Eliciting and Analyzing Life History Narratives. *Journal of Aging Studies, 4*: 17–29.

Luken, P. C. (1987). Social Identity in Later Life: A Situational Approach to Understanding Old Age Stigma. *International Journal of Aging and Human Development, 25*: 177–193.

Luckman, B. (1970). The Small Life Worlds of Modern Man. *Social Research, 37*: 580–596.

Luscher, K. (1974). Time: A Much Neglected Dimension in Social Theory and Research. *Sociological Analysis and Theory, 4*: 101–117.

Mandler, J. (1984). *Stories, Scripts and Scenes: Aspects of Schema Theory.* Hillsdale, NJ: Lawrence Erlbaum.

Manheimer, R. (1989). The Narrative Quest in Qualitative Gerontology. *Journal of Aging Studies, 3*: 253–262.

Marcus, G. & Fischer, M. (Eds.) (1986). *Anthropology as Cultural Critique: An Experimental Moment in the Human Sciences.* Chicago, IL: University of Chicago Press.

Marshall, V. W. (1979). No Exit: A Symbolic Interactionist Perspective on Aging. *International Journal of Aging and Human Development, 9*: 345–358.

Maxwell, R. J. (1972). Anthropological Perspectives. In H. Yaker, H. Osmond, & F. Cheeik (Eds.), *The Future of Time* (pp. 36–72). New York: Anchor Books.

McClusky, H. Y. (1971). *Education: Background and Issues* (p. 9). White House Conference on Aging. Washington, DC: U.S. Government Printing Office.

McCulloch, A. W. (1980). What Do We Mean by "Development" in Old Age. *Ageing and Society, 1*: 230–245.

Mead, G. H. (1934). *Mind, Self and Society.* Chicago, IL: University of Chicago Press.

Mergler, N., & Schleifer, R. (1985). The Plain Sense of Things: Violence and the Discourse of the Aged. *Semiotica, 54* (1/2): 177–199.

Mergler, N., & Goldstein, M. (1983). Why Are There Old People? Senescence as Biological and Cultural Preparedness for the Transmission of Information. *Human Information, 26*: 72–90.

Meyerowitz, J. (1984). The Adult Child and the Childlike Adult. *Daedalus, 113* (3): 19–48.

Midwinter, E. (1982). *Age is Opportunity: Education and Older People.* London: Centre for Policy on Ageing.

Miller, G. (1973). Ends, Means and Galumphing. *American Anthropologist, 75*: 87–97.

Moody, H. R. (1988). Towards a Critical Gerontology: The Contribution of the Humanities to Theories of Aging. In J. E. Birren & V. L. Bengtson (Eds.), *Emergent Theories of Aging.* New York: Springer.

Moore, S. F. (1978). Old Age in a Life-Term Social Arena: Some Chagga of Kilimanjaro in 1974. In: B. Myerhoff & A. Simic (Eds.), *Life's Career—Aging: Cultural Variations on Growing Old* (pp. 23–76). Beverly Hills, CA: Sage Publications.

Moore, S., & Myerhoff, B. (Eds.), (1977). *Secular Ritual.* Assen: Van-Gorcum.

Myerhoff, B. (1978a). *Number Our Days.* New York: Dutton.

Myerhoff, B. (1978b). A Symbol Perfected in Death: Continuity and Ritual in the Life and Death of an Elderly Jew. In A. Simic & B. Myerhoff (Eds.), *Life's Career, Aging.* Beverly Hills, CA: Sage Publications.

Myerhoff, B. (1982). Life History Among the Elderly: Performance, Visibility and Re-Membering. In J. Ruby (Ed.), *A Crack in the Mirror: Reflexive Perspectives in Anthropology.* Philadelphia, PA: University of Pennsylvania Press.

Myerhoff, B. (1984). Rites and Signs of Ripening. In D. I. Kertzer & J. Keith (Eds.), *Age and Anthropological Theory.* London: Cornell University Press.

Myerhoff, B., & Simic, A. (Eds.) (1978). *Life's Career—Aging: Cultural Variations on Growing Old.* Beverly Hills, CA: Sage Publications.

Neugarten, B. L. (1972). Personality and the Aging Process. *The Gerontologist* (Spring). [Reprinted in: S. H. Zarit (Ed.), *Readings in Aging and Death: Contemporary Perspectives* (pp. 72–77). New York: Harper & Row, 1977.]

Norris, C. (1985). *Deconstruction: Theory and Practice*. London: Methuen.

Norton, D. (1984). The University of the Third Age—Nationwide. In E. Midwinter (Ed.), *Mutual Aid Universities* (pp. 107–126). London: Croom Helm.

Nussbaum, J. F. (1989). *Life-Span Communication: Normative Processes*. Hillsdale, NJ: Lawrence Erlbaum.

Ortner, S. (1984). Theory in Anthropology since the Sixties. *Comparative Studies in Society and History, 26*: 126–165.

Oyer, H., & Oyer, E. (1976). *Aging and Communication*. Baltimore, MD: University Park Press.

Pels, P., & Nancel, L. (1991). Introduction: Critique and the Deconstruction of the Anthropological Authority. In P. Pels, & L. Nancel (Eds.), *Constructing Knowledge* (pp. 1–22). London: Sage Publications.

Penn, J. (1972). *Linguistic Relativity vs. Innate Ideas*. Bloomington, IN: Bloomington University Press.

Perlmutter, M. (1983). Learning and Memory through Adulthood. In N. White Riley, B. B. Hess, & K. Bond (Eds.), *Aging in Society: Selected Reviews of Recent Research* (pp. 219–242). Hillsdale, NJ: Lawrence Erlbaum.

Philibert, M. (1984). Contemplating the Development of Universities of The Third Age. In E. Midwinter (Ed.), *Mutual Aid Universities* (pp. 51–71). London: Croom Helm.

Philipson, C. (1982). *Capitalism and the Construction of Old Age*. London: Macmillan.

Pike, K. (1954). *Language in Relation to a Unified Theory of the Structure of Human Behavior*. Vol. 1.

Polanyi, L. (1989). *Telling the American Story*. Cambridge, MA: The MIT Press.

Radcliffe, D. (1984). The International Perspective for U3As. In E. Midwinter (Ed.), *Mutual Aid Universities* (pp. 61–71). London: Croom-Helm.

Raz, A. E. (1992/1993). The Reinherited Self: A Case Study in the Dynamics of a Social World. In N. K. Denzin (Ed.), *Studies in Symbolic Interaction*. Greenwich CT: JAI Press.

Reder, L. M., Wible, C., & Martin, J. (1986). Differential Memory Changes with Age: Exact Retrieval versus Plausible Inference. *Journal of Experimental Psychology: Learning, Memory and Cognition, 12*: 72–81.

Ricouer, P. (1991) {1986}. *From Text to Action: Essays in Hermeneutics, II*. Evanston, IL: Northwestern University Press.

Rogers, M. F. (1983). *Sociology, Ethnomethodology and Experience: A Phenomenological Critique*. Cambridge, U.K.: Cambridge University Press.

Rosow, I. (1974). *Socialization to Old Age*. Berkeley, CA: University of California Press.

Rossi, I. (1983). *From the Sociology of Symbols to the Sociology of Signs: Towards a Dialectical Sociology*. New York: Columbia University Press.

Roth, J. (1962). *Timetables*. Indianapolis, IN: Bobbs-Merrill.

Rowles, G. D. (1978). *Prisoners of Space?* Boulder, CO: Westview Press.

Rowles, G. D., & Ohta, R. J. (1981). *Aging and Milieu.* New York: Academic Press.

Roy, D. (1959). Banana Time: Job Satisfaction and Informal Interaction. *Human Organization, 18*: 158–168.

Rubinstein, R. L. (1992). Anthropological Methods in Anthropological Research: Entering the Realm of Meaning. *Journal of Aging Studies, 6*: 57–66.

Ruby, J. (Ed.) (1982). *A Crack in the Mirror: Reflexive Perspectives in Anthropology.* Philadelphia, PA: University of Pennsylvania Press.

Sahlins, M. (1976). *Culture and Practical Reason.* Chicago, IL: University of Chicago Press.

Said, E. (1978). *Orientalism.* New York: Random House.

Sanjek, R. (1990). On Ethnographic Validity. In R. Sanjek (Ed.), *Fieldnotes* (pp. 385–419). Ithaca, NY: Cornell University Press.

Schopenhauer, A. (1844 [1818]). *Die Welt als Wille und Vorstellung.*

Schutz, A. (1972). Choice and the Social Sciences. In L. E. Embree (Ed.), *Life Worlds and Consciousness: Essays for Aron Gurevitch* (pp. 565–590). Evanston, IL: Northwestern University Press.

Schutz, A., & Luckman, T. (1973). *The Structure of the Life World.* Evanston, IL: Northwestern University Press.

Searle, J. (Ed.) (1979). *Expressions and Meaning.* Cambridge, U.K.: Cambridge University Press.

Shattuck, R. (1980). *The Forbidden Experiment.* London: Quartet Books.

Shibutani, T. (1955). Reference Groups as Perspectives. *American Journal of Sociology, 60*: 562–568.

Shotter, J. &, Gergen, K. (Eds.) (1989). *Texts of Identity.* London: Sage Publications.

Shweder, R. A., & Miller, J. (1985). The Social Construction of the Person: How Is It Possible?" In K. Gergen, & D. Keith (Ed.), *The Social Construction of the Person* (pp. 41–53). New York: Springer-Verlag.

Silverman, P. (Ed.) (1987). *The Elderly as Modern Pioneers.* Bloomington, IN: Indiana University Press.

Simmons, L. (1945). *The Role of the Aged in Primitive Society.* New Haven, CT: Anchor Books.

Smelser, N., & Erikson, E. (Eds.) (1980). *Themes of Love and Work in Adulthood.* Cambridge, MA: Harvard University Press.

Sokolovsky, J., & Cohen, C. (1981). Being Old in the Inner City: Support Systems of the SRO Aged. In L. Fry (Ed.), *Dimensions: Aging, Culture and Health* (pp. 163–184). New York: J. F. Bergin Publishers.

Sperber, D. (1975). *Rethinking Symbolism.* Cambridge, U.K.: Cambridge University Press.

Stevens, W. (1954). *Collected Poems.* New York: Knopf.

Stewart, F. (1976). *Fundamentals of Age-Group Systems.* New York: Academic Press.

Strathern, M. (1987). Out of Context: The Persuasive Fictions of Anthropology. *Current Anthropology, 28* (3, June): 252–281.

Strauss, A. (1961). *Images of the American City.* New York: The Free American Press.

Strauss, A. (1962). Transformations of Identity. In A. Rose (Ed.), *Human Behaviour and Social Processes* (pp. 63–85). Boston, MA: Houghton Mifflin.

Strauss, A. (1967). Strategies for Discovering Urban Theory. In L. F. Schnore & H. Fagin (Eds.), *Urban Research and Policy Planning.* Beverly Hills, CA: Sage Publications.

Strauss, A. (1978). A Social World Perspective. In: N. K. Denzin (Ed.), *Studies in Symbolic Interaction,* Vol. 1 (pp. 119–128). Greenwich, CT: JAI Press.

Strauss, A. (1982). Social Worlds and Legitimation Processes. In N. K. Denzin (Ed.), *Studies in Symbolic Interaction,* Vol. 4 (pp. 171–190). Greenwich, CT: JAI Press.

Strauss, A. (1987). *Qualitative Analysis for Social Scientists.* Cambridge, U.K.: Cambridge University Press.

Titmuss, R. M. (1970). *The Gift Relationship: From Human Blood to Social Policy.* London: George Allen & Unwin.

Tobin, S. S., & Lieberman, M. A. (1976). *Last Home for the Aged.* San Francisco, CA: Jossey-Bass.

Trevarthen, C., & Logotheri, K. (1989). Child in Society, and Society in Children: The Nature of Basic Trust. In S. Howell & R. Willis (Eds.), *Societies at Peace: Anthropological Perspectives.* London: Routledge.

Tufte, V., & Myerhoff, B. (1975). Life History as Integration: Personal Myth and Aging. *The Gerontologist, 15*: 541–543.

Turnbull, C. M. (1984). *The Human Cycle.* London: Jonathan Cape.

Turner, B. S. (1984). *The Body and Society.* Oxford: Blackwell.

Turner, B. S. (1987). Aging, Dying and Death. In *Medical Power and Social Knowledge* (pp. 11–31). Newbury Park, CA: Sage Publications.

Turner, V. (1969). *The Ritual Process.* Chicago, IL: Aldine.

Turner, V. (1975). *Dramas, Fields and Metaphors: Symbolic Action in Human Society.* Ithaca, NY: Cornell University Press.

Turner, V. (1977). Variations on a Theme on Liminality. In S. F. Moore & B. Myerhoff (Eds.), *Secular Ritual* (pp. 36–52). Amsterdam, Assen: Van Gorcum.

Turner, V. (1978). Foreword. In B. Myerhoff, *Number Our Days.* New York: Dutton, 1978.

Unruh, D. (1983). *Invisible Life: The Social Worlds of the Aged.* Beverly Hills, CA: Sage Publications.

Van-Gennep, A. (1960 [1908]). *The Rites of Passage* (trans. M. B. Visedom & G. L. Caffee). Chicago, IL: University of Chicago Press, Phoenix Books.

Veron, E. (1990). Entre Pierce et Bateson: Une Certaine Idée du Sens. In Y. Winkin (Ed.), *Bateson: Premier État d'un Héritage* (pp. 171–183). Paris: Éditions du Seuil.

Vesperi, M. (1985). *City of Green Benches*. Ithaca, NY: Cornell University Press.

Vietor, K. (1950). *Goethe: The Thinker*. Cambridge, MA: Harvard University Press.

Wagner, R. (1986). *Symbols That Stand for Themselves*. Chicago, IL: University of Chicago Press.

Whorf, B. (1956). *Language, Thought and Reality*. New York: Wiley.

Winner, E. (1990). *The Point of Words: Children's Understanding of Metaphor and Irony*. Cambridge, MA: Harvard University Press.

Wittgenstein, L. (1953). *Philosophical Investigations*. Oxford: Basil Blackwell.

Woodward, K. (1980). *At Last, the Real Distinguished Thing: The Late Poetry of Eliot, Pound, Stevens and Williams*. Columbus, OH: Ohio State University Press.

Woodward, K. (1991). *Aging and Its Discontents*. Bloomington, IN: Indiana University Press.

Wyatt-Brown, A. M. (1989). The Narrative Imperative: Fiction and the Aging Writer. *Journal of Aging Studies, 3*, 1: 55–67.

Yeats, W. B. (1971). *The Variorum Edition of the Poetry of W. B. Yeats* (ed. D. Allt & S. Alspach). New York: Macmillan.

Zarit, S. H. (Ed.) (1977). *Readings in Aging and Death: Contemporary Perspectives*. New York: Harper & Row.

Zerubavel, E. (1985). *The Seven Day Circle*. New York: The Free Press.

Zola, I. K. (1982). *Missing Pieces*. Philadelphia, PA: Temple University Press.

Index

About the Author

HAIM HAZAN is Professor of Sociology and Anthropology at Tel Aviv University. He is the author of several books including *The Limbo People* (1979), *A Paradoxical Community* (1990), *Managing Change in Old Age* (1992), and *Old Age: Constructions and Deconstructions* (1994).

ISBN 0-89789-462-6

90000>

EAN

9 780897 894623

HARDCOVER BAR CODE